Foreword

Welcome to Jill Walker's "Caribbean Cookbook". As you can see this is a cookbook with a difference as it is full of Jill's splendid drawings of island scenes and local foods. We hope you will enjoy both the recipes and the drawings, whether you are buying it for yourself, receiving it as a gift or giving it to a friend.

Jill's first cookbook, "Cooking in Barbados", also fully illustrated, has been a great success, being reprinted many times since it was first published in 1983.

Over the years, Jill's lovely tropical products, including her many pen and wash prints, have become internationally known. Now recipes from around the Caribbean together with her drawings are incorporated in this illustrated cookbook.

Based on the first cookbook, this "Caribbean Cookbook" has many more recipes and many more drawings. Opposite we have acknowledged our friends throughout the region who have helped compile the recipes.

As in the first cookbook, the idea has been to select recipes which are likely to prove family favourites, and which contain ingredients generally available world-wide or for which substitutes can be readily found. We have carefully tried and tested every recipe. Each of those we selected for this cookbook we enjoyed tasting and we hope you will enjoy them too.

Charlotte Hingston

D1551217

Contents

For each Section we have high-lighted below some of our particularly favourite recipes, which you may like to try first.

Appetisers and Soups

Flying Fish Pâté

6 flying fish fillets
2 tbsp cream cheese
Mayonnaise to bind

Salt and pepper
Lime or lemon juice
Dash Tabasco sauce

Poach the fish in water for about 15 minutes until tender. Flake the fish and add the cream cheese and enough mayonnaise to bind the fish together. Season with the salt, pepper, lime or lemon juice and Tabasco sauce, pack into a small bowl and chill. Serve with toast and salad as an appetiser or serve on biscuits with drinks.

Tropical Rarebit

2 tbsp (1 oz) margarine
1 cup (4 oz) grated cheese
4 large bananas mashed
1 egg yolk beaten
¼ tsp mustard

Salt and pepper
Parsley chopped
Chives chopped
6 slices bread for toasting
Butter for toast

Melt the margarine over a low heat then add the cheese and banana, stirring until the cheese melts and the mixture is well blended. Stir in the egg and mustard and season to taste with salt and pepper. Cook gently for a further few minutes, stirring continuously. Set aside to cool. When the banana mixture is cool, make the toast, butter it and cut into squares. Spread the pieces with the banana topping, sprinkle with parsley and chives and brown under a hot grill for a minute. Makes about 24 squares to serve with drinks.

Avocado Dip

1 large or two small avocados
Juice of half a lime or lemon
2 blades chives chopped
   or 1 tsp grated onion

4 tbsp mayonnaise
Dash Worcestershire sauce
Pinch of salt

Halve the avocado, scoop out the flesh and mash it. Stir in the lime or lemon juice, chives or onion, mayonnaise, Worcestershire sauce and salt. Serve with biscuits or potato crisps. Unless eaten immediately avocado dip should always be chilled or frozen with the stone in it to prevent discolouration. Remove the stone just before serving.

Did you know that .....
Avocado Pears originated in Mexico. Unlike most vegetables which contain less than 1% fat, avocados contain up to 17% – so weight watchers beware! An avocado is ripe when the centre of the broader end gives slightly when pressed and the stone rattles when the pear is gently shaken. Large avocados can weigh up to 2lbs.

Cuba

Haiti Dominican Republic

Jamaica

C A R I B B E A N   S E A

Fishermen by the Caribbean Sea

Breadfruit Chips

Piece of breadfruit   **Oil for deep frying**
Salt

Peel the breadfruit and cut it into slices like a melon. Remove the core and cook the breadfruit lightly in salted water, about 15 minutes. When cooked cut each slice crossways into wedges and deep fry until golden brown. Drain, and sprinkle with salt.

Curried Coconut

Coconut   **Curry powder**

Cut the coconut into thin slices. Sprinkle with curry powder and serve with drinks. To see how to prepare a coconut turn to the Coconut Crisps recipe on page 10.

Salt Fish Balls

¾ cup (5 oz) salt cod   **1 small onion grated**
** cooked and flaked**   **Black pepper**
2 eggs beaten   **Oil for deep frying**
½ cup (¼ pt) milk

Mix all the ingredients together and roll into marble sized balls, adding a few breadcrumbs if the mixture will not roll neatly. Deep fry until golden brown, drain on absorbent paper and then serve on cocktail sticks with drinks.

Chicken and Rum Pâté

1 lb chicken livers   **¼ cup (3 tbsp) rum**
½ lb pork sausage meat   **Chives, thyme and parsley, chopped**
½ lb onion chopped   **Salt and pepper**
2 cloves garlic crushed   **2 slices streaky bacon**
Oil for frying   **Salad to garnish**
1 egg

Lightly fry the chopped onions and crushed garlic in a little oil, then put aside in a bowl to cool. Add the livers to the pan and cook over a low heat until they are still just a little pink in the middle. Allow to cool. Prepare a 7" x 3" loaf tin by lining the bottom with the bacon slices. When the cooked ingredients are cool blend them and all the remaining ingredients in a liquidiser. Blend until the pâté reaches the desired degree of smoothness and then turn the mixture into the prepared tin. Place the tin in a slightly larger shallow container and fill the outer one with water. Bake at 375°F, 190°C, GM 5 for 1 hour. Cool in the tin before turning out and garnishing with salad. Serves 12 generously.

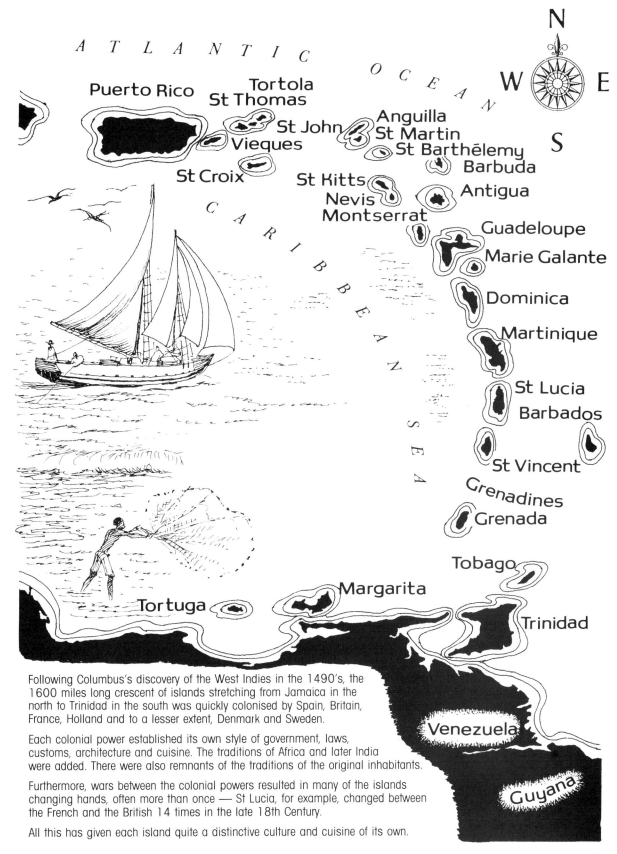

ATLANTIC OCEAN

CARIBBEAN SEA

N
W E
S

Puerto Rico
Tortola
St Thomas
St John
Vieques
St Croix
Anguilla
St Martin
St Barthélemy
Barbuda
St Kitts
Nevis
Montserrat
Antigua
Guadeloupe
Marie Galante
Dominica
Martinique
St Lucia
Barbados
St Vincent
Grenadines
Grenada
Tobago
Margarita
Trinidad
Tortuga
Venezuela
Guyana

Following Columbus's discovery of the West Indies in the 1490's, the 1600 miles long crescent of islands stretching from Jamaica in the north to Trinidad in the south was quickly colonised by Spain, Britain, France, Holland and to a lesser extent, Denmark and Sweden.

Each colonial power established its own style of government, laws, customs, architecture and cuisine. The traditions of Africa and later India were added. There were also remnants of the traditions of the original inhabitants.

Furthermore, wars between the colonial powers resulted in many of the islands changing hands, often more than once — St Lucia, for example, changed between the French and the British 14 times in the late 18th Century.

All this has given each island quite a distinctive culture and cuisine of its own.

9

Coconut Crisps

Coconut   **Salt**

Use the following method to free the white flesh of a coconut. Pierce the three "eyes" at the end of the coconut with a skewer and drain off the "milk" (it makes a refreshing cool drink). Bake the coconut at 375°F, 190°C, GM 5 for 20 minutes, then break it open with a hammer and ease out the flesh with a knife. To make Coconut Crisps, trim off the brown surface and cut the coconut into long thin pieces with a potato peeler. Lay the pieces in a single layer on a baking tray and brown lightly under the grill. Sprinkle with salt and serve with drinks.

Crispy Christophene

2-3 christophenes

Christophenes, when peeled, leave a sticky residue on your hands. To avoid this rub your hands lightly with oil beforehand. Peel the christophenes, halve them and discard the cores. Slice thinly with a potato peeler and chill in a bowl of water for about 12 hours. They will then be crisp with a slightly sweet apple taste. Sprinkle with celery salt to serve with drinks. Crispy Christophenes can also be used in salads, sliced to use with dips or used instead of apple in fruit salads. (Christophenes have no calories).

Plantain Chips

2 half-ripe plantains   **Salt**
Oil for deep frying

Slice the plantains diagonally into ⅛" thick slices. Chill in iced water for 30 minutes and then dry the slices on absorbent paper. Deep fry until golden brown and crispy. Sprinkle with salt and serve with drinks.

Dolphin Dip

1 large dolphin steak   **Parsley chopped**
Salt and pepper   **Dash Worcestershire sauce**
½ cup (4 oz) cream cheese   **2 tbsp mayonnaise**
Juice of 1 lime or ½ a lemon   **A little milk**
3 blades chives chopped

Poach the fish in water for 15-20 minutes and allow it to cool. Flake it finely and season with salt and pepper. Mix the cream cheese, lime or lemon juice, chives, parsley, Worcestershire sauce and mayonnaise and add it to the fish. Thin to a creamy consistency with either a little more mayonnaise or milk. Garnish with parsley or chives and serve with biscuits, potato crisps or Crispy Christophene slices (see recipe above).

Christophene

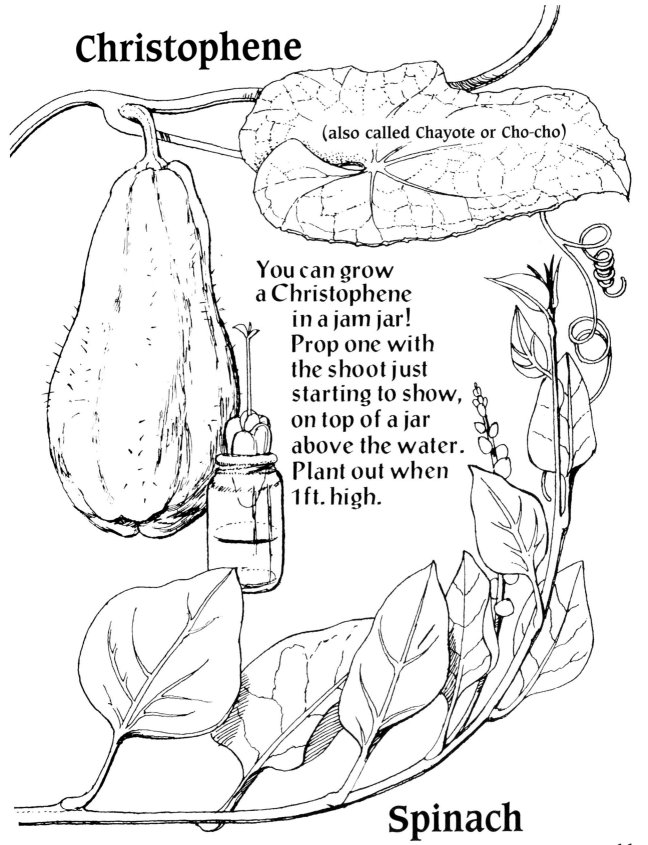

(also called Chayote or Cho-cho)

You can grow
a Christophene
in a jam jar!
Prop one with
the shoot just
starting to show,
on top of a jar
above the water.
Plant out when
1ft. high.

Spinach

Crab Backs

2 cups (½ lb) crab meat, flaked
2 tsp butter and 2 tsp oil
1 small onion finely chopped
1 small clove garlic crushed
2 tsp chives finely chopped
¼ tsp ground cloves
¼ tsp ground nutmeg

¼ tsp hot pepper sauce
½ tsp thyme
2 tsp Worcester sauce
1 tbsp rum
2 tsp lime or lemon juice
½ cup (1 oz) fresh breadcrumbs
Salt and pepper

Fry the onion in the butter and oil, then add the garlic and fry for a further minute. Stir in all the remaining ingredients except the crab meat and ⅓ of the breadcrumbs. Cook for 2 minutes and then stir in the crab meat. Fill 4 crab backs (or scallop shells or ramekin dishes), sprinkle the remaining breadcrumbs over the top and bake at 375°F, 190°C, GM 5 for 30 minutes until browned. Garnish and serve hot or cold. Serves 4.

Paw-Paw Fruit Cream

2 medium paw-paws (papayas)
Juice of 1 lime or ½ a lemon
1 tbsp cornflour
1 cup (½ pt) orange juice

1 egg yolk
3 tbsp sugar
Grated coconut

Peel the paw-paws, halve them and remove the seeds. Slice the flesh and arrange it in individual bowls, sprinkling it with the lime or lemon juice. To make the cream, dissolve the cornflour in a little orange juice. Beat the egg yolk and sugar until pale and pour it into a small pan with the orange juice and cornflour. Bring to the boil and stir until it thickens. Cool, then pour over the paw-paw and serve chilled, sprinkled with coconut. Serves 6.

Breadfruit Vichyssoise

2 tbsp (1 oz) margarine
2 medium onions chopped
1 clove garlic crushed
1 cup (½ lb) chopped breadfruit

3 cups (1½ pts) chicken stock
1 small carton natural yoghurt
Salt and pepper
3 blades chives chopped

Fry the onion and garlic in the margarine. Peel and chop the breadfruit, discarding the core. Add the breadfruit and stock to the onion and garlic. Cover and simmer until the breadfruit is tender, about 15 minutes. Cool it, then add the yoghurt and liquidise until smooth. Season with salt and pepper and chill. Garnish with chopped chives. Serves 6.

Did you know that .....
Captain Bligh was en route from the Pacific with 1,000 breadfruit plants when the famous 1787 mutiny on the "Bounty" occurred. He introduced breadfruit to the West Indies in 1792.

Bringing in the Fish

13

Pigeon Pea Soup

2 cups (1 pt) pigeon peas
5 cups (2½ pts) chicken stock
2 cups (1 lb) cubed pumpkin
2 onions finely chopped

1 clove garlic crushed
1 green pepper chopped
Salt and pepper
Parsley chopped

Peel and chop the pumpkin into ½" cubes. Combine all the ingredients except the salt, pepper and parsley in a large pan. Cover and simmer until the peas are tender and the pumpkin begins to disintegrate and thickens the soup, about 25 minutes. Season with salt and pepper and serve garnished with parsley. Green peas can be used if pigeon peas are not available. Serves 6-8.

Chilled Avocado Soup

2 large or 4 small avocados
Juice of 1 large lime or
  ¾ of a lemon
2 cups (1 pt) chicken stock

1 small carton of natural yoghurt
Salt and pepper
3 blades chives chopped

Halve the avocados, remove and reserve their stones and scoop the flesh from the skins. Liquidise the avocado with the lime or lemon juice, the stock and yoghurt. Season with salt and pepper and return the avocado stones to the soup to prevent it discolouring. Chill the soup, removing the stones before serving. Serve garnished with chives. Serves 4.

Chilled Cream of Cucumber Soup

3 cucumbers of 8" long
1 medium onion chopped
3 cups (1½ pts) chicken stock
Salt and pepper

3 tsp cornflour
1 small carton of natural yoghurt
1 cup (½ pt) milk
2 blades chives chopped

Peel and roughly chop the cucumbers. Simmer them with the onion in the stock for about 15 minutes. Cool slightly and then liquidise. Strain it and return it to the pan and season with salt and pepper. Mix the cornflour in a tablespoonful of the soup and then add it to the pan. Simmer, without boiling and stirring occasionally, until slightly thickened. Stir in the milk and half the yoghurt and chill. Serve in individual bowls, into which a tablespoonful of the remaining yoghurt has been swirled, and garnish each serving with chives. Serves 6.

Did you know that .....
Pigeon pea bushes are about 8' tall and are often grown along the edge of fields. Even in the same pod peas can be green, brown, cream or mauve in colour. Some islands call Pigeon peas Gunga peas.

Picking Pigeon Peas

15

Pumpkin Soup

⅓ cup (2 oz) split peas
4 cups (2 pts) ham or
  chicken stock
1 onion chopped
1½ cups (¾ lb) chopped pumpkin

1 slice bacon fried and crumbled
Salt and pepper
Mixed herbs
Parsley chopped

Soak the split peas overnight. Rinse the split peas and add them to the stock with all the other ingredients except the parsley. Simmer until the pumpkin and split peas are tender and then liquidise. Reheat and serve garnished with parsley. Serves 6.

Eddoe Soup

1 lb eddoes
¾ cup (4 oz) salt beef or pork
¾ cup (4 oz) minced beef
3 onions chopped

Salt and pepper
1-2 tsp thyme
1 tbsp butter
Parsley chopped

Peel and halve the eddoes, chop the salt meat and bring both to the boil in 8 cups (4 pts) of water. Add the minced beef and onion and cook for about 20 minutes, until the eddoes are tender. Liquidise the eddoe mixture, add the salt, pepper and thyme, and simmer for 5 minutes. Stir in the butter and garnish with parsley. Serves 10.

Callaloo Soup

1 lb callaloo leaves, spinach,
  chinese cabbage or swiss chard
¾ cup (4 oz) salt pork or
  6 slices lean bacon
5 cups (2½ pts) chicken stock
1 onion chopped
1 clove garlic crushed
3 spring onions chopped

¼ tsp thyme
1¼ cups (½lb) crab meat or
  white fish fillets
8 young okras sliced
1 tbsp butter
Salt and pepper
1 green pepper sliced

Chop the greens roughly and cut the pork or bacon into ½″ pieces. Simmer these in the stock with the onion, garlic, spring onions and thyme until the pork or bacon is tender, about 20 minutes. Add the flaked crab or white fish and the okras and cook until the okras are tender, about 15 minutes. Stir in the butter and season to taste with salt and pepper. Garnish with green pepper slices. Serves 10.

Did you know that .....
Callaloo leaves are the young leaves from the dasheen or taro family of root vegetables. They should not be eaten raw as they can make you unwell.

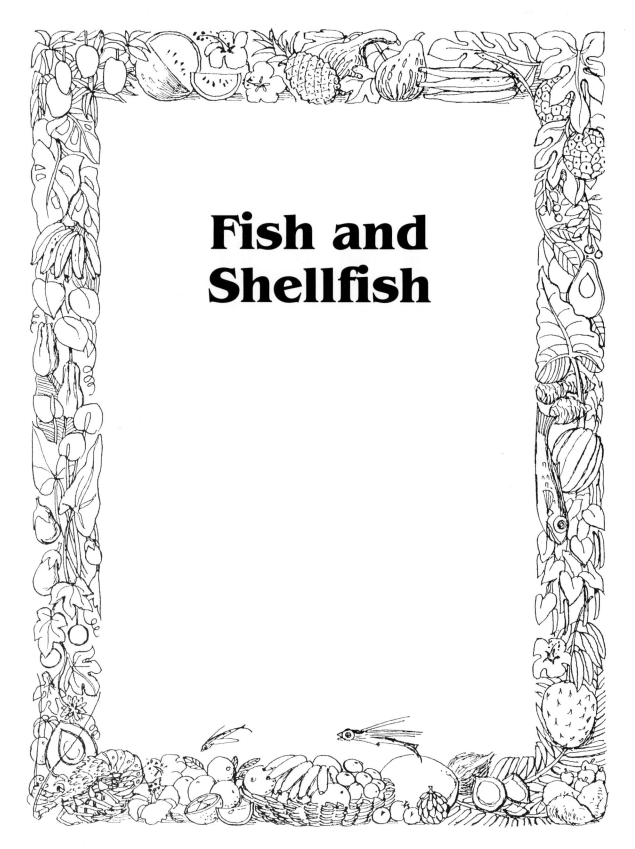

Fish and Shellfish

Dolphin Bake

4 dolphin or other white
   fish steaks
Juice of 1 lime or ½ a lemon
Salt and pepper
⅓ cup (3 oz) butter
1½ lb spinach or 1¼ lb
   swiss chard

1 large onion finely chopped
1 clove garlic crushed
¼ cup (1 oz) flour
1 cup (½ pt) milk
2 tomatoes sliced
1 cup (4 oz) grated cheese
Paprika

Rinse the fish steaks and place them on a baking tray. Sprinkle them with the lime or lemon juice, salt and pepper, and dot with a third of the butter. Cover tightly with foil and bake at 350°F, 180°C, GM 4 for 20 minutes. Meanwhile cook the spinach in boiling water for 3-4 minutes, or the swiss chard for 8 minutes. When cooked, drain thoroughly (squeezing out all the water) and chop it finely. Melt half the remaining butter and gently cook the onion and garlic, cool slightly and stir into the chopped greens. Arrange the greens in a lightly greased baking dish. When the fish is cooked remove the skin and bones and arrange the chunks of fish on top of the greens. Make the sauce with the remaining butter, the flour and milk, adding in the juices from the fish. Pour the sauce over the fish and make a decorative overlapping line of tomatoes on top. Sprinkle with grated cheese and paprika. Brown under the grill or bake at 425°F, 220°C, GM 7 for 8-10 minutes until golden and bubbling. Serves 4.

Stir-Fried Octopus

1½ lbs octopus sliced
   into ¼" strips
2 tbsp cooking oil
6 spring onions chopped,
   with leaves included
1½ cups (4 oz) bean sprouts
2 sticks celery finely chopped

1 tbsp finely chopped fresh ginger
1 green pepper thinly sliced
2 chinese cabbage leaves thinly sliced
2 cloves garlic crushed
Salt and pepper
3 tbsp sweet sherry
Lime or lemon wedges to garnish

Heat the oil in a wok or a very large and heavy frying pan. When the oil is very hot drop in the strips of octopus and stir-fry it for two minutes. Quickly add all the vegetables and stir-fry for a further 1½ minutes. Season with salt and pepper and add the sherry, stirring all the time. Serve immediately, accompanied by rice or noodles, and garnished with the wedges of lime or lemon. Serves 4.

Preparing Octopus: Octopus is generally sold prepared for cooking, but if not this is how to do it. (Squid is prepared the same way, and can be used as an alternative to octopus). Pull out the head and all the attachments including the ink bag and discard. Wash the sac and tentacles under running water for several minutes then beat it like a steak to tenderise it. Slice the tentacles into ¼" strips and the sac into ¼" rings. Blanch them in boiling water for a few minutes, then drain and peel off the skin.

OCTOPUSES are found in holes in the coral reefs.

ST LUCIA

Dolphin Quiche

9″ pie shell unbaked,
using 1½ cups (6 oz) flour
3 dolphin or other white
fish steaks
1 tbsp chopped celery
1 tbsp chopped parsley
1 tbsp chopped onion

2 tbsp dry sherry
4 eggs
1½ cups (¾ pt) cream or
evaporated milk
Salt and pepper
¼ tsp ground nutmeg

Prick the base of the unbaked pie shell thoroughly and bake for 10 minutes at 400°F, 200°C, GM 6. Allow to cool. Poach the fish in water for 15 minutes, then flake it, discarding the skin. To make the filling, combine the celery, parsley, onion, sherry and fish and spread it over the base of the pie shell. Beat the eggs and add the cream or evaporated milk, salt, pepper and nutmeg. Pour this over the fish. Bake at 425°F, 220°C, GM 7 for 35-40 minutes reducing the temperature to 375°F, 190°C, GM 5 for the last 15 minutes. The quiche is cooked when a knife inserted into the centre comes out clean. Serves 6.

Baked Red Snapper or Dolphin

6 red snapper or dolphin steaks
Juice of 1 lime or ½ a lemon
3 onions sliced
1 eggplant (aubergine) cubed
4 tomatoes chopped
6 blades chives chopped

2 cloves garlic crushed
2½ cups (1¼ pts) milk
3 tbsp flour
1½ tbsp butter
Dash of Angostura Bitters
Salt and pepper

Skin and rinse the fish steaks, sprinkle them with salt and rub well with the lime or lemon juice. Place the steaks in a lightly greased baking dish and surround them with the onion, eggplant, tomato, chives and garlic. Gradually add the milk into the flour, a little at a time, stirring to keep it smooth. Add the chopped butter, Angostura Bitters, salt and pepper to the sauce and then pour it over the fish. Bake uncovered at 350°F, 180°C, GM 4 for about 50 minutes until the fish is cooked and lightly browned on top. Serves 6.

Did you know that .....
King fish is a game fish which weighs up to 100 lbs and can leap 10 feet out of the water. Its meat is inclined to be slightly dry. The Spanish Mackerel is related to the King fish. It can weigh up to 50 lbs but is usually found weighing about 3 lbs. Dolphin, with its easily recognisable flat-shaped head, is also a West Indian game fish, weighing up to 30 lbs. Along with the Red Snapper its meat is one of the most tasty in the Caribbean. The Red Snapper can weigh 20 lbs but is more usually found weighing about 6-8 lbs. It feeds on crabs and small fish. The Albacore Bonito is often considered the choice fish in the Tuna family. Its usual weight is 8-12 lbs although some of the fish in this family may reach as much as 600 lbs.

Well-known Caribbean Fish

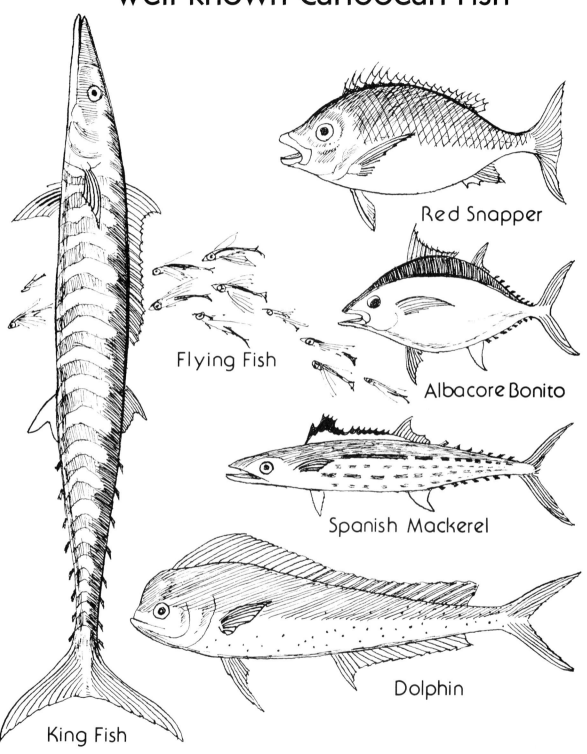

Red Snapper

Flying Fish

Albacore Bonito

Spanish Mackerel

Dolphin

King Fish

Seafood Tart

⅓ cup (3 oz) margarine
1½ cups (6 oz) plain flour
3 tbsp sesame seeds toasted
3 dolphin or other white
   fish steaks
½ cup (¼ pt) milk
1 bay leaf
2 tbsp (1 oz) margarine

2 tbsp plain flour
1 egg beaten
1 hard boiled egg chopped
½ cup (2 oz) peeled prawns
   or shrimps
Salt and pepper
1 tbsp French mustard

Rub the first two quantities of margarine and flour together. Add the sesame seeds and enough cold water to bind the mixture into a dough. Chill for 10 minutes and then roll it out and line a 9″ pie dish. Chill for a further 10 minutes and then bake at 350°F, 180°C, GM 4 for 10 minutes, and then allow it to cool. Poach the fish steaks in the milk with the bay leaf for 10 minutes. Strain off the milk and reserve it. Flake the fish, discarding the skin. Melt the remaining margarine and stir in the last of the flour. Gradually add the reserved milk, stirring all the time, and cook for 2 minutes. Remove from the heat and stir in the beaten egg, the hard boiled egg, fish and prawns or shrimps. Season to taste. Spread the mustard over the inside of the pie shell and pour in the sauce mixture. Bake at 375°F, 190°C, GM 5 for 25-30 minutes until lightly browned. Serves 6.

Cold Dolphin with Avocado Sauce

4-5 lb piece of dolphin or
   other white fish
Juice of 1 lime or ½ a lemon
3 tbsp (1½ oz) butter
Pepper
1 onion sliced

For the sauce:
2 large or 4 small avocados
Juice of 1 lime or ½ a lemon
3 tbsp vegetable oil
1 tsp salt
Pepper to taste

Wash the fish and place it on a large piece of foil. Brush the lime or lemon juice and butter over both the inside and outside of the fish. Sprinkle it with pepper and put 4 table-spoonfuls of water and the onion around the base. Wrap the foil closely around the fish and bake it at 350°F, 180°C, GM 4 for about 30 minutes. When the fish is cooked, remove and discard the skin, allow the fish to cool, and then chill it. Place the cooked onion inside the fish. Beat all the remaining ingredients together to make the sauce. Unless the sauce is to be used immediately one avocado stone should be placed in it to prevent discolouration. Before serving cover the fish with half of the sauce and serve the rest separately. Garnish with a selection of parsley, cucumber, lettuce, radishes and wedges of lime. Serves 6.

Did you know that .....
In the Caribbean, dolphin is the name of a delicious game fish. Visitors are often concerned that it refers to the well-known porpoise-like mammal, but it does not!

Fish Market by the Sea

Salt Fish and Ackee

1 lb salt cod
2 dozen ackees or 18 oz tin
¾ cup (4 oz) lean salt pork
   finely diced
A little oil for frying
2 medium onions finely chopped
1 green pepper chopped
1 clove garlic crushed

1 tsp finely chopped hot pepper seeded
4 spring onions chopped
¼ tsp thyme
3 tomatoes peeled and chopped
Freshly ground black pepper
Tomatoes, parsley or watercress
   to garnish

Salt Fish and Ackee is considered the national dish of Jamaica. Soak the salt cod in cold water for at least 8 hours. Drain it and simmer in fresh water until tender, 20-25 minutes. If fresh ackees are available, add them to the fish 15 minutes before it is cooked. Drain, and separate the ackees. Remove any bones and skin from the fish then flake it and return it to the ackees. In a large pan fry the salt pork in the oil until it is lightly browned, then add the onion, green pepper and garlic and fry until the onion is soft. Add the hot pepper, spring onions, thyme and tomatoes and cook for a further 4-5 minutes. Now add the cooked cod (patted dry with kitchen towel) and the ackees. If tinned ackees are used drain them well and add them to the dish at this point. Ensure all the ingredients are heated through, then serve seasoned with freshly ground black pepper and garnished with a selection of tomato, parsley and watercress. Serves 4-6.

Barbequed Red Snapper

Red snapper or portion
   of other fish for 2
2 cloves garlic crushed

Juice of 2 limes or 1 lemon
Salt and pepper
Sprig of thyme

Usually portions of fish are bought ready for cooking, but if not ensure it is gutted, descaled and washed before marinating. Lay the fish on a plate. Combine the garlic, lime or lemon juice, salt and pepper in a small bowl. Spoon this marinade over both the outside and inside of the fish and put the sprig of thyme inside it. Leave to marinate for about two hours. If you are going to barbeque the fish cook it on a grill close to the coals. Cook for about 25 minutes, until the fish will flake easily off the bone. Turn it once and brush it regularly with the remains of the marinade and a little butter. If a barbeque is not possible the fish can be cooked in the oven. To do so marinate the fish on a large double piece of foil and then wrap the foil tightly round it for baking. Bake at 375°F, 190°C GM 5 for 25 minutes. Steaks of fish are also convenient to barbeque or bake in this way. Serves 2.

Did you know that .....
Jamaica's luxuriant vegetation includes about 3,000 species of flowering plants and over 550 varieties of fern. Originally the island was totally forested and the Arawak Indians called it "Xaymaca", land of wood and water. Today 6% remains covered in well-stocked forest.

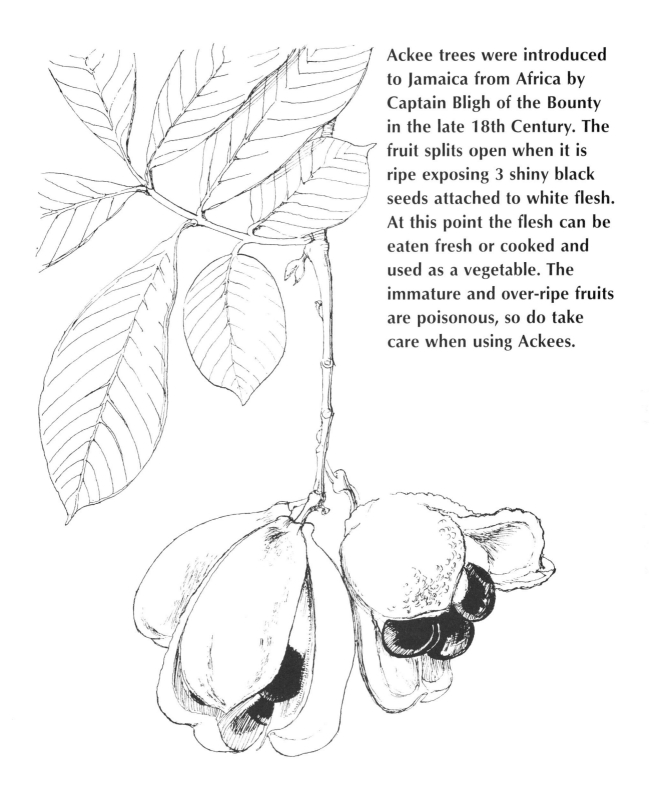

Ackee trees were introduced to Jamaica from Africa by Captain Bligh of the Bounty in the late 18th Century. The fruit splits open when it is ripe exposing 3 shiny black seeds attached to white flesh. At this point the flesh can be eaten fresh or cooked and used as a vegetable. The immature and over-ripe fruits are poisonous, so do take care when using Ackees.

JAMAICAN ACKEE

25

Flying Fish Barbados Style

8 flying fish or other white
  fish fillets
1 small onion grated
1 small green pepper chopped
1 blade chives chopped
Thyme and parsley

Salt and pepper
A few drops of lime or lemon juice
1 egg beaten
Breadcrumbs
Oil for frying
Lime or lemon slices

Mix the seasoning ingredients and spread over the meaty side of the fish. Leave for about 1 hour. Dip the fish into the beaten egg and then into the breadcrumbs. Fry gently in a little oil for about 10 minutes. Drain the fish on kitchen paper and serve garnished with the slices of lime or lemon. This style of fried flying fish is traditionally served with "Rice and Peas" (see page 66), and it also makes a delicious buffet dish served cold. Serves 4-6.

Spicy Fish with Rice

4 dolphin or other
  white fish steaks
1½ cups (9 oz) rice
3 tsp salt, ½ tsp pepper

2 medium onions chopped
1 clove garlic crushed
¼ cup (2 oz) margarine
2 tbsp cooking oil

Cook the rice for 15 minutes in 3 cups (1½ pts) of water with 2 teaspoonfuls of salt. Fry the onion and garlic in the margarine and oil for 10 minutes, stirring occasionally. Cut the fish into 1″ pieces and discard the skin. Add the fish, pepper and remaining salt to the onion and cook for 5 minutes, stirring once or twice. Add the drained rice and cook for a further 5 minutes stirring frequently. Adjust the seasoning before serving. Serves 6.

Flying Fish Pie

8 flying fish or other white
  fish fillets
4-6 courgettes thinly sliced
Salt and pepper
6 tomatoes peeled and sliced

2 onions finely chopped
2 cloves garlic crushed
1¼ cups (7½ oz) brown rice cooked
2 tbsp parsley chopped
4 tbsp fresh herbs chopped

For the sauce:
3 tbsp (1½ oz) margarine
3 tbsp (1½ oz) flour

2 cups (1 pt) milk
¾ cup (3 oz) grated cheese

Lightly grease a large baking dish and arrange the sliced courgettes around the sides and base. Slice the fish into strips and add to the dish, seasoning well with salt and pepper. Add the sliced tomatoes. Lightly cook the onion and garlic in a little oil, then stir in the cooked rice, parsley and herbs. Add the rice mixture into the baking dish and level the top. Make the cheese sauce and pour it over the pie, decorating the top with a little more parsley or grated cheese. Bake at 400°F, 200°C, GM 6 for 30 minutes. Serves 6.

Flying Fish

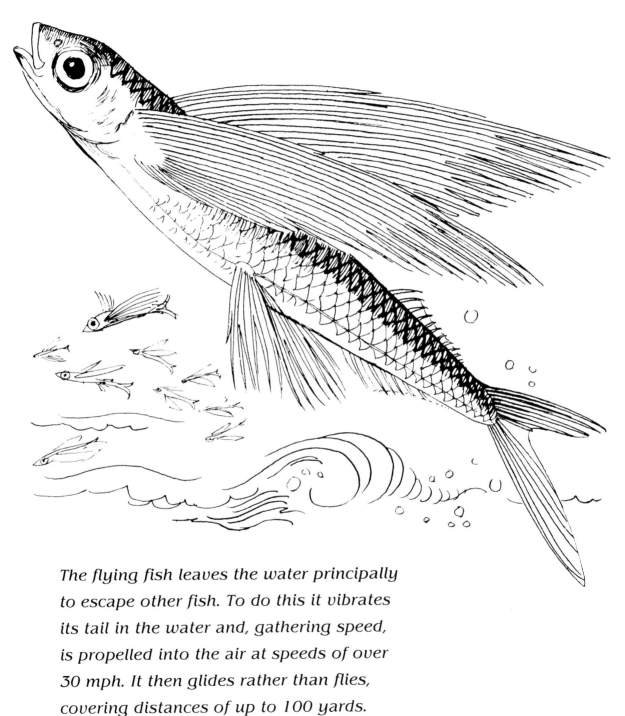

*The flying fish leaves the water principally
to escape other fish. To do this it vibrates
its tail in the water and, gathering speed,
is propelled into the air at speeds of over
30 mph. It then glides rather than flies,
covering distances of up to 100 yards.*

Pickled Conch Souse

3 medium conchs (lambi)
1-2 onions thinly sliced
1 green pepper finely chopped
7" cucumber peeled and sliced
1 clove garlic crushed

1-2 tomatoes chopped
Salt and pepper
Hot pepper sauce to taste
Juice of 6-8 limes or
   3-4 lemons

In some islands, conch is known as lambi. The conch should be very fresh and uncooked. Clean well, pound to tenderise it and slice it thinly. Combine all the ingredients in a bowl, being a little cautious with the hot pepper sauce to start with – it's very hot! The lime or lemon juice should just cover the conch and the seasonings. Marinate for at least 4 hours, or overnight in the fridge, turning the ingredients occasionally. Should the lime or lemon flavour be too strong it can be diluted by adding a little olive oil or water.

This pickling recipe can also be used for fresh fish, for example king fish, dolphin or grouper, and in French speaking islands it is called Ceviche.

Crab and Prawn Pancakes

The pancakes:
2 cups (8 oz) flour
1 tsp salt

2 eggs
2 cups (1 pt) milk

Sieve the flour and salt, make a well in the centre and add the eggs and half the milk. Slowly beat until it forms a smooth mixture, then add the remaining milk and leave to stand for two hours. This is enough batter for 12-15 pancakes of 8" diameter.

The sauce:
3 tbsp (1½ oz) margarine
⅓ cup (1½ oz) plain flour
1 tsp English mustard

2 cups (1 pt) milk
1 cup (4 oz) grated cheese
1 tbsp chopped parsley

Melt the margarine over a gentle heat, smooth in the flour and cook for a minute. Add the mustard, then remove the pan from the heat and gradually add the milk, stirring constantly until smooth. Return the pan to the heat stirring as the sauce thickens, then add the cheese and parsley.

The filling:
3 cups (¾ lb) crab meat fresh,
   tinned or frozen

3 cups (¾ lb) peeled prawns fresh,
   tinned or frozen

Mix the crab and the prawns with a little salt and pepper and enough of the cheese sauce to give a firm but creamy consistency. Make the pancakes in an 8" heavy base frying pan, greased with a small amount of olive oil. Spread the filling evenly over the cooked pancakes, then roll up the pancakes and arrange them in an oven proof serving dish. Top with the remaining cheese sauce and brown under the grill before serving. Serves 6.

CONCHS

being prepared
in St Martin

Lobster Casserole

1 large lobster cooked
1 tbsp butter
1 tbsp flour
1 cup (½ pt) milk
10¾ oz tin condensed cream of
   mushroom soup

Parsley chopped
Salt and pepper
¼ tsp ground nutmeg
½ cup (¼ pt) dry sherry
4 tbsp grated cheese

Cut the lobster meat into small pieces. Melt the butter and blend in the flour. Slowly stir in the milk and then the mushroom soup and cook for a few minutes until smooth and thickened. Add the lobster pieces, parsley, salt, pepper, nutmeg and sherry to the sauce and stir well. Turn the mixture into a lightly greased baking dish and sprinkle with the grated cheese. Bake at 375°F, 190°C, GM 5 for 30 minutes. Serves 6.

Shrimp Soufflé

1½ cups (6 oz) peeled shrimp,
   finely chopped
3 tbsp (1½ oz) butter
1 tbsp grated onion
4 tbsp flour
¾ cup (⅓ pt) milk

Salt and pepper
Ground nutmeg
Juice of 1 lime or ½ a lemon
4 egg yolks beaten
6 egg whites

Cook the onion gently in the melted butter for 2-3 minutes. Add the flour and mix well. Add the milk a little at a time, stirring until the mixture thickens. Season with salt, pepper, nutmeg and lime or lemon juice. Remove from the heat and stir in the lightly beaten egg yolks and the shrimp. Beat the egg whites until stiff and stir the first half into the shrimp mixture and then fold the second half in very gently. Pour into a lightly greased soufflé dish and bake at 375°F, 190°C, GM 5 for 35-40 minutes until golden, light and fluffy. Shrimp soufflé is very good served with rice and a fish based sauce with nutmeg and sherry added. Serves 4.

Did you know that .....
There are two varieties of lobster. The large one, which grows to over 20 lbs, comes from the waters off North America and Europe. The smaller variety comes from tropical American waters, the Indian Ocean and the Mediterranean Sea. It grows to 4 lbs in size and is known as the Spiny or Rock lobster. It is really a member of the crayfish family, lacking the distinctive big claws of the true lobster. Small lobsters usually have the best flavour and the average 1-2 lb lobster is considered a serving for one. The Spiny lobster is known in the Mediterranean and the French Antilles as Langouste. Lobster should not be deep frozen for more than a month.

Shrimp Soufflé

Spiny Lobster
For Lobster Casserole

Curried King Fish

4 king fish or other
   white fish steaks
2 medium onions sliced
2 tbsp curry powder
Oil for frying
3 tbsp flour

Salt and pepper
1 eggplant (aubergine) cubed
8 oz tin chopped tomatoes
1 cup (8 oz) cubed pumpkin
1 clove garlic crushed
½ cup (¼ pt) fish or chicken stock

Fry the onion and curry powder in a large pan and set aside. Divide the fish into small sections, discarding the skin. Dip the fish pieces in the seasoned flour and fry them until golden brown. Return the onion and curry to the pan and add the eggplant, tomatoes, pumpkin, garlic and stock. Cover and simmer gently until the eggplant is tender and the pumpkin disintegrates to thicken the gravy, about 25 minutes. Serves 4.

Lobster Salad

2 cups shelled, cooked lobster
2 sticks celery finely chopped
1 tbsp finely chopped
   capers (optional)
½ cup (¼ pt) mayonnaise

2 tbsp ketchup
Salt and pepper
1 large banana, thinly sliced
Lettuce
Paprika

Mix together all except the last three ingredients. Add the banana slices just before serving to avoid them discolouring. Arrange the lettuce decoratively on a flat dish and turn the lobster salad onto it. Sprinkle with paprika to garnish. This is also a quick and delicious dish if two tins of tuna is substituted for lobster. Serves 4.

Yam Fish Cakes

6 dolphin or other
   white fish steaks
1 medium onion chopped
Salt and pepper
1 lb yams or sweet potatoes
½ cup (¼ pt) milk

1 egg beaten
2 tbsp parsley chopped
½ cup (2 oz) flour
Shortening for deep frying
Parsley to garnish

Poach the fish in water for about 20 minutes, adding the onion, salt and pepper. Peel the yams or sweet potatoes, chop them roughly and cook for about 20 minutes, until they are tender. When they are cooked, drain and mash them until smooth, then add the milk. Flake the fish, discarding the skin, and add it to the yam or sweet potato with the beaten egg and parsley. Mix well and adjust the seasoning. Divide into 12 equal portions and form into flat, round fish cakes. Sprinkle both sides of them with flour and fry in the shortening until browned and crispy. Drain on absorbent paper and garnish with parsley to serve. Serves 6.

Chicken

Curried Chicken and Mango

4 chicken breasts
½ cup (2 oz) flour
1½-2 tbsp curry powder
¼ cup (2 oz) margarine
½ cup (¼ pt) milk
½ cup (¼ pt) chicken stock
Salt and pepper
2 ripe medium mangoes
3 tbsp grated coconut or
    chopped parsley to garnish

Cut the chicken into thin slices, toss in the flour and fry with the curry powder in the margarine for 5 minutes, turning frequently. Gradually stir in the milk and the stock, add the salt and pepper and bring to the boil, simmering for 2-3 minutes. Peel the mangoes and cut them into ½″ strips and arrange them in a casserole. Season them with salt and pepper and then add the curried chicken mixture on top. Bake at 400°F, 200°C, GM 6 for 30 minutes until the sauce is bubbling and the mango is tender. Garnish with grated coconut or parsley and serve with rice. Serves 4.

Pineapple Chicken

6 chicken pieces
Juice of 1 lime or
    ½ a lemon
Salt and pepper
¼ tsp ground cloves
2 tbsp margarine
2 onions sliced
2 cloves garlic crushed
3 tomatoes peeled and chopped
3 tbsp raisins
1 bay leaf
1 bonnie pepper seeded and chopped
    or ½ tsp hot pepper sauce
1 cup (½ pt) chicken stock
1 small pineapple or a tin
    of pineapple chunks
3 tbsp rum
½ tsp cornflour
Parsley to garnish

Rub the chicken pieces with the lime or lemon juice, salt, pepper and ground cloves, then fry them in the margarine until lightly browned and set aside. Using the same pan, fry the onion and garlic until the onion is soft, then add the tomatoes, raisins, bay leaf and bonnie pepper or hot pepper sauce, and simmer for 5 minutes. (When chopping bonnie peppers hold them with a knife and fork rather than with your fingers as they will cause the skin to burn for about 2 hours). Add the chicken pieces and the stock, stir lightly and simmer for 20 minutes until the chicken is tender.

To make the pineapple mixture to accompany the chicken, first prepare the pineapple by peeling and coring it, then chop it roughly and put it and its juice aside in a saucepan. Take ½ cup (¼ pt) of the liquid that the chicken is cooking in and add it to the saucepan with the chopped pineapple or pineapple chunks. Bring it to the boil and cook uncovered, stirring occasionally, until the liquid reduces to about half, then add the rum. Thicken if necessary with a little cornflour. Pour the mixture over the chicken, stir lightly and cook for 2-3 minutes more. Arrange the chicken pieces in a serving dish, pour the pineapple over the chicken and garnish with a sprig of parsley. Serves 6.

Chickens to market — Antigua Style!

Rum and Grapefruit Chicken

4 chicken pieces
2 tbsp flour
Salt and pepper
¼ cup (2 oz) margarine

2 tbsp rum
½ cup (¼ pt) chicken stock
4 tbsp sherry
1 grapefruit

Coat the chicken in the seasoned flour. Fry in the margarine until golden brown and then reduce the heat, cover and cook for about 20 minutes until tender. When the chicken is cooked drain off the fat, pour the rum over the chicken and ignite it. When the flames subside lift the chicken pieces out, place on a serving dish and keep it hot. Add the stock and sherry to the pan and season with salt and pepper. Halve the grapefruit and squeeze the juice from one half into the stock. Cook this sauce until reduced to about half quantity, stirring it occasionally, then add the segments from the other half of the grapefruit and pour over the chicken before serving. Serves 4.

Chicken in Orange Sauce

6 chicken pieces
3 tbsp flour
Salt and pepper
Oil for frying
2 cups (1 pt) orange juice

2 tbsp white vinegar
2 tbsp brown sugar
1 tsp ground nutmeg
2 cloves garlic crushed
2 oranges segmented

Coat the chicken pieces in the seasoned flour. Fry them in the oil until golden brown on both sides and then transfer them to a casserole. Add the orange juice, vinegar, sugar, nutmeg and garlic. Stir to mix the ingredients, cover and simmer for about 45 minutes until the chicken is tender. Garnish with the orange segments and cook for a further 5 minutes. Serves 6.

Did you know that .....

Citrus came to the New World with Columbus's arrival in Haiti in 1493. By 1525 a travelling naturalist wrote of the great abundance of citrus on that island. Grapefruit originated in Barbados. It first appeared there in the late 1700s in the island's lush inland gullies. It is a cross between a Sweet Orange and a Shaddock. The Shaddock (or Pummelo) is a less well known citrus; it is large and slightly pear-shaped with a thick rind and white or pink flesh. It is named after a Captain Shaddock who first brought it to Barbados.

Lemons and limes are frequently used in cooking throughout the Caribbean. When grown commercially they are picked when mature but still green. This is because their acid content is highest at that time so they will store longest. A useful tip is that both lemon and lime juice can be used to remove the smell of garlic from the hands.

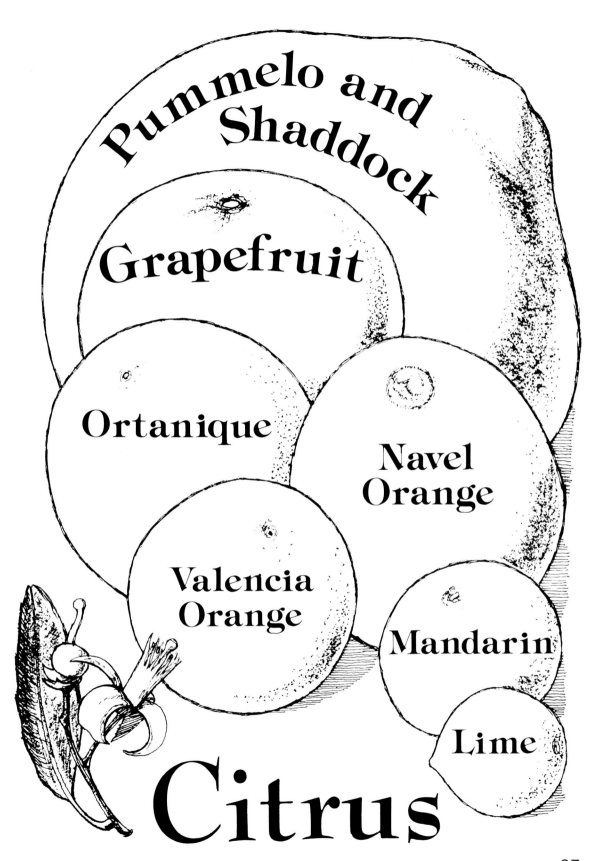

Pummelo and Shaddock

Grapefruit

Ortanique

Navel Orange

Valencia Orange

Mandarin

Lime

Citrus

Flambé Haitian Chicken

1 large roasting chicken
Salt and pepper
1½ tbsp honey

⅓ cup (4 tbsp) orange juice
2 tbsp rum

For the stuffing:
1½ cups (¾ pt) cooked rice
3 bananas mashed
2½ tbsp raisins
Pinch of ground nutmeg
Pinch of ground ginger

Juice and grated rind of
 1 orange
1 tbsp rum
Salt and pepper

Prepare the chicken by rinsing it and patting dry with kitchen paper. Make the stuffing by combining all the stuffing ingredients, then fill the chicken with it. Place the chicken in a roasting tin and sprinkle with a little salt and pepper. Dissolve the honey in the orange juice and brush it all over the chicken, then pour the remaining juice into the roasting tin. Roast at 350°F, 180°C, GM 4 for 1½-2 hours, basting it occasionally with the juices in the tin. When cooked, place the chicken on a carving board, pour over the rum and ignite it just before serving. Serves 6.

Chicken Flamingo

4 chicken breasts
Salt and pepper
1 tbsp margarine
About 5 fresh guavas, or
 8 oz of tinned or stewed guavas

1 tbsp grated fresh ginger
½ cup (¼ pt) chicken stock
Chopped chives to garnish

Season the chicken breasts with salt and pepper. Melt the margarine and fry the chicken gently and covered for 20-25 minutes, until cooked through and lightly browned on all sides. In the meantime prepare the guava sauce. If using fresh guavas, peel off their fine skin, halve them and scoop out the seeds. If using tinned guavas just drain the juice off. Simmer the guava shells and the grated ginger in the chicken stock for about 20 minutes, and when the guavas are soft liquidise the guava mixture. When the chicken is cooked place it on a serving dish, pour over the guava sauce and garnish with chopped chives. Serves 4.

Did you know that .....
The island of Hispaniola is shared by two countries, the Republic of Haiti and the Dominican Republic. Haiti occupies just over one third of the island, to the western end. Together with Puerto Rico and Cuba, Haiti and the Dominican Republic are the main Spanish speaking countries of the Caribbean. In Santo Domingo, the capital of the Dominican Republic, is the first cathedral founded in the New World, and in it are the alleged remains of Columbus.

Cutting down coconuts in the inland hills, where the St Vincent parrot is found.

(Maranta Arundinacea)

ST VINCENT ARROWROOT

is used throughout the world for thickening sauces and also in baby foods. The root contains an easily digested form of starch.

Chicken and Eggplant Casserole

4 chicken pieces
4 slices streaky bacon
1 onion sliced
1 green pepper sliced
1 medium eggplant (aubergine),
   cut into ¼" thick sticks

1½ cups (¾ pt) chicken stock
Salt and pepper
½ tsp mixed herbs
2 tbsp tomato purée
1 tbsp cornflour

Fry the bacon and when some of its fat has melted add the onion and the green pepper. Add a little margarine if more fat is needed. When the bacon is cooked and the onion and pepper lightly browned put it in a casserole. Brown the chicken pieces in the same pan then add them to the casserole along with the eggplant, stock, salt, pepper, herbs and tomato purée. Stir the ingredients lightly, cover and bake at 350°F, 180°C, GM 4 for 45 minutes. To thicken the gravy blend the cornflour with 2 tablespoonfuls of water and stir it into the casserole, cooking it for a further 10 minutes. Serves 4.

Chicken with Crusty Sweet Potato Top

6 chicken breasts cooked
   and cubed
6 small onions cooked
1 piece pumpkin lightly cooked
   and cubed
1 cup (½ pt) pigeon peas or
   green peas cooked

1 tbsp chopped parsley
Salt and pepper
3 tbsp flour
3 tbsp (1½ oz) margarine
¾ cup (⅓ pt) chicken stock
¾ cup (⅓ pt) milk
1 tbsp sherry (optional)

Sweet Potato Crust:
¾ cup (3 oz) flour
1 tsp salt
1 tsp baking powder

2 cups (1 pt) sweet potato cooked,
   mashed and cooled
6 tbsp (3 oz) margarine

Combine the chicken, onions, pumpkin, peas, parsley, salt and pepper and place in a baking dish. Smooth the flour and margarine together in a small pan over a low heat and slowly stir in the stock and the milk. Cook for a few minutes until thickened, then add the sherry and pour over the chicken mixture.

Sweet Potato Crust: Sift the dry ingredients together and mix in the sweet potato. Rub in the margarine to make a smooth dough. Roll the dough out to fit inside the top of the baking dish and lay it on top of the chicken mixture. Bake at 350°F, 180°C, GM 4 for about 45 minutes until golden brown and crispy. Serves 6.

Did you know that .....
When a field of sweet potatoes is being gathered you can dig up your own by buying a "hole" or plant, entitling you to as many potatoes as that particular sweet potato vine has produced.

Sweet Potato Carts

*The leaves are heaped over the sweet potatoes
to keep the sun off them.*

Spicy Chicken Salad

Chicken for 6 cooked and cubed
1 green pepper chopped
2 tbsp grated onion
3 sticks celery chopped
½ cup (¼ pt) French dressing
Mayonnaise to bind

Curry powder to taste
Salt and pepper
1 grapefruit segmented,
    preferably a pink one
7" cucumber
Parsley chopped

Combine the cubed chicken, green pepper, onion, celery and French dressing. Marinate for about 12 hours in the fridge and then pour off any dressing which has not been absorbed. Mix the mayonnaise and curry powder and stir into the chicken mixture, using enough mayonnaise to bind the chicken together. Add salt and pepper to taste. Just before serving add the grapefruit segments and then the peeled cucumber, either cubed or made into balls using a melon scoop. Serve chilled, garnished with parsley. Serves 6.

Cucumber Chicken Salad

Chicken for 6 cooked and cubed
7" cucumber
½ cup (¼ pt) chicken stock
½ cup (¼ pt) milk
Juice of 1 lime or ½ a lemon

1 tsp castor sugar
Salt and pepper
Cayenne pepper (optional)
3 blades chives chopped

Peel the cucumber, cut it into chunks and simmer in a little salted water for 5 minutes and then drain. Make a thick white sauce with the chicken stock and the milk. Add the white sauce, lime or lemon juice, sugar, salt, pepper and cucumber to the cubed chicken and mix well. Serve chilled, sprinkled with cayenne pepper and garnished with chopped chives. Serves 6.

Saucy Tomato Chicken

4 chicken breasts
1 onion thinly sliced
1 carrot thinly sliced
1 slice bacon chopped
1 tbsp margarine
1 heaped tsp flour

1 medium tin tomatoes
½ tsp mixed herbs
Salt and pepper
1 cup (½ pt) chicken stock
1 cup (4 oz) grated cheese

Fry the onion, carrot and bacon in the margarine until lightly browned. Add the flour and cook for another minute. Add the tomatoes, herbs and stock and season with salt and pepper. Bring to the boil and simmer uncovered for an hour. Cool, and then liquidise to form the sauce. Season the chicken with a little salt and pepper. Put half the sauce in a casserole, add the chicken pieces and then the rest of the sauce. Cover and bake for 30 minutes at 350°F, 180°C, GM 4, sprinkling with the cheese after 20 minutes. Serves 4.

Chickens for Sale

Savoury Stuffed Chicken Pieces

4 chicken pieces
1 medium onion grated
½ green pepper finely chopped
1 blade chives chopped
Thyme and parsley

Salt and pepper
Juice of ½ a lime or lemon
1 egg beaten
Breadcrumbs
Oil for frying

This is a good recipe to cook or re-heat at barbeques. Chicken drumsticks are probably the easiest choice to eat in the fingers; this quantity of ingredients will be enough for about 8 medium drumsticks. Mix all the seasoning ingredients. Make 2-3 slits in each piece of chicken and fill with a little seasoning, rubbing any extra over the outside. Leave for about 1 hour. Dip each piece of chicken into the beaten egg and then into the breadcrumbs. Fry in the oil until golden brown then reduce the heat, cover and cook for a further 20 minutes until tender. Serves 4.

Banana Chicken

4 chicken pieces
2 tbsp flour
1 tsp salt
4 tsp curry powder

Oil for frying
2-3 bananas
1 cup (6 oz) rice
2-3 limes or 1-2 lemons

The combination of hot curry and the sweetness of fried bananas makes this a most distinctive dish. Mix the flour, salt and curry powder and coat the chicken with it. Fry the chicken in the oil until golden brown and then reduce the heat, cover and cook for a further 15 minutes until tender. Halve the bananas and add them to cook for 5 minutes. Meanwhile cook the rice in boiling salted water for about 20 minutes until tender, adding a slice of lime or lemon to the water. To serve spread the rice on a serving dish, arrange the chicken and banana pieces on top and garnish with slices of lime or lemon. Serves 4.

Chicken and Okra Casserole

4 chicken pieces
½ cup (4 oz) margarine
1 lb small okras,
  with stems removed

2 cloves garlic crushed
¼ tsp ground cloves
1 cup (½ pt) tomato juice
Salt and pepper

Fry the whole okras in the margarine for 5 minutes, then set them aside. Put the chicken pieces in the pan and brown both sides. Add the garlic and cloves, cover and cook gently for 20 minutes, turning the chicken pieces once. Add in the tomato juice, 1 cup (½ pt) of water, salt and pepper, and lastly add the okras. Cover and simmer gently for 45 minutes. Serve gently to avoid breaking the okras. Serves 4.

Meats

Barbequed Ginger Pork

8 pork chops
1 tbsp brown sugar
1 tbsp olive or vegetable oil
2 tbsp grated fresh ginger
¼ tsp mixed spice

1 tbsp hoisin sauce
2 tbsp soy sauce
1 clove garlic crushed
2 tbsp green ginger wine (optional)

Place the pork chops in a shallow dish. Combine all the other ingredients as a marinade and pour over the pork. Cover and chill in the fridge for a few hours or overnight. To cook, barbeque or grill the chops for about 10 minutes, turning once and basting regularly with the marinade. Serves 4.

Lamb and Eggplant Casserole

1 lb lean lamb minced
  or chopped
1¼ cups (7½ oz) rice
2 medium eggplants
  (aubergines)

3 tbsp salad oil
2 onions chopped
1½ tsp salt
1 tsp pepper
1½ tsp cinnamon

Cook the rice in boiling salted water until tender, about 20 minutes. Peel the eggplant and cut it into ¼" slices. Brown the slices on both sides in half the oil, then set them aside. Add the remaining oil to the pan with the lamb, onion, salt, pepper and cinnamon. Cook for 10 minutes, stirring frequently. Lightly grease a large casserole and arrange the rice, lamb and eggplant in alternate layers until all is used, ending with a layer of rice on top. Cover and bake at 375°F, 190°C, GM 5 for 35 minutes. Serves 4.

Lamb Kebabs with Orange Spice Sauce

1½ lb shoulder of lamb
Piece of pumpkin
  (for about 16 1" cubes)
4-6 small onions
Salt and pepper
Cooking oil

¾ cup (6 oz) brown sugar
1 cup (½ pt) orange juice
4 tsp Worcestershire sauce
Juice of 1 lime or ½ a lemon
1 tsp mustard
1 tbsp flour

Cook the pumpkin lightly, about 12 minutes. Cube the lamb and quarter the onions. Thread the lamb, onion and pumpkin alternately onto 12"-18" skewers. Season and brush with the oil. Place over a barbeque or under the grill and cook for 10-15 minutes turning occasionally. To make the sauce, combine all the remaining ingredients and bring to the boil, stirring continuously until smooth and thickened. Pour the sauce over the kebabs and serve with hot white rice and salad. Serves 4.

Kebabs can be barbequed

GINGER

Ginger is the rhizome of *Zingiber Officinale*. To prevent them starting to grow after being harvested they are exposed to the sun or are dipped in hot water.

Spicy Pork Creole

2 lb boneless pork
2 tbsp (1 oz) margarine
2 sticks celery chopped
1 onion chopped
½ a green pepper chopped
1 tomato chopped
1 clove garlic crushed

Salt and pepper
1 cup (½ pt) chicken stock
¼ cup (3 tbsp) barbeque sauce
¼ cup (3 tbsp) molasses
Dash Angostura bitters
1 tbsp cornflour

Slice the pork into pieces ½" thick and brown it in the margarine along with the celery, onion and pepper. Then add all the remaining ingredients except the cornflour, cover and simmer until the pork is tender, about 25-35 minutes. To thicken the gravy, blend the cornflour to a paste in ½ cup (¼ pt) of water and stir it into the pork about five minutes before cooking is finished. Good served with rice. Serves 6.

Lime and Ginger Chops

8 lamb chops
4 tbsp cooking oil
Grated rind and juice of
  2 limes or 1 lemon

1 tbsp brown sugar
1½ tsp ground ginger
Salt and pepper

Marinate the lamb chops in a mixture of all the other ingredients for 2-3 hours, turning them occasionally. Cook the chops under a hot grill or on a barbeque for 15 minutes, turning them three times and basting them frequently with the marinade. Serves 4.

Tropical Breadfruit Lasagne

½ a small breadfruit
1 lb minced beef
1 onion finely chopped
1 small eggplant (aubergine)
  chopped
½ a green pepper chopped
2 cloves garlic crushed

2 tbsp (1 oz) margarine
14½ oz tin chopped tomatoes
1 tbsp tomato purée
1 tsp hot pepper sauce
Salt and pepper
1 cup (½ pt) white sauce
¾ cup (3 oz) grated cheese

Peel the breadfruit and slice it into pieces ¾" thick. Parboil the slices for 10 minutes. Meanwhile fry the onion, eggplant, green pepper and garlic in half the margarine for 10 minutes. Set this aside, melt the remaining margarine and fry the meat for 10 minutes until browned. Now add the cooked onions, eggplant, green pepper and garlic, along with the tomatoes, tomato purée, hot sauce, salt and pepper. Mix well, cover and simmer for 5 minutes. Make the white sauce and then layer the meat, breadfruit and white sauce in a large baking dish. Sprinkle the top with grated cheese and bake for 35 minutes at 325°F, 160°C, GM 3, until bubbling and golden brown. Serves 4.

BREAD FRUIT

Spicy Creole Beef

2 lbs casserole beef, cut into strips 1½" long
3 tbsp (1½ oz) butter
3 bay leaves

½ tsp ground nutmeg
2 tbsp rum
Salt and pepper

For the Marinade:
Juice of 2 limes or 1 lemon
4 cloves garlic crushed
2 tsp grated fresh ginger

2 tsp cinnamon
1 tsp ground cloves
1 bonnie pepper seeded and chopped

This is a dish typical of the French speaking islands. Combine all the marinade ingredients in a large bowl. (When chopping bonnie peppers hold them with a knife and fork rather than with your fingers as they cause the skin to burn for about 2 hours). Add the meat to the marinade, stirring well to ensure it is well coated. Cover and put in the fridge to marinate for 24 hours or more. When the meat is ready to cook, melt the butter in a heavy casserole and then add the meat and the marinade. Cook for about 10 minutes, stirring to brown the meat all over. Add the remaining ingredients, cover and simmer very gently for 1½-2 hours until the meat is tender. Stir occasionally. Good served with rice and salad. Serves 4-6.

Lamb Curry

2 lbs boneless lamb, in 1" cubes
2 tsp freshly ground black pepper
Flour
2 tbsp vegetable oil
2 tbsp margarine
2 onions finely chopped
2 cloves garlic crushed
2 tbsp chopped fresh lemon grass

1 tsp grated fresh ginger
2 tsp chopped fresh coriander
½ tsp ground cumin
½ tsp ground nutmeg
Grated rind of 1 lime or ½ a lemon
1 green pepper chopped
2 cups (1 pt) lamb stock

Accompaniments:
Grated coconut
Raisins or sultanas
Chutneys

Thin slices of banana
Chopped pineapple
Thin slices of cucumber

This is a mild curry with lots of spicy flavours. Toss the lamb in flour, then heat the oil in a large pan. When the oil is hot add the meat, stirring frequently to brown it on all sides and then set the meat aside. Discard any excess oil, lower the heat and melt the margarine in the same pan. Add all the remaining ingredients except the lamb stock and stir over a medium heat for about 3 minutes. Return the lamb to the pan with the spicy mixture, add the stock and cook gently for about 45 minutes until the lamb is tender. Serve with rice and a selection of the traditional accompaniments to curry suggested above. Serves 4.

Barbados Black Belly Sheep

Stuffed Plantains

¾ lb minced beef
3 large ripe plantains (their skins
   are nearly black when ripe)
6 slices streaky bacon
2 onions chopped
1 clove garlic crushed

1 green pepper chopped
2 tomatoes chopped
½ tsp oregano
Salt and pepper
2 eggs beaten
Oil for deep frying

Fry the bacon until crispy and then set it aside. Cut the plantains into four lengthways so that they form twelve long, thin strips, and sauté them in the bacon fat until they are soft and golden. Carefully drain them on absorbent paper and when they are cool enough to handle shape each strip into a circle and secure with a cocktail stick. To make the filling, brown the mince in the bacon fat and then add the onion, garlic, green pepper, tomato, oregano, salt, pepper and the crumbled bacon. Cook until the onion and green pepper are soft, about 20 minutes. Fill each plantain circle with the stuffing, dip them into the beaten egg and deep fry in oil, turning once to brown both sides. Serves 4-6.

West Indian Roast Pork

5-6 lb loin of pork
1 tsp salt
½ tsp pepper
½ tsp ground cloves
1 tsp ground ginger
2 cloves garlic crushed

2 bay leaves crumbled
¾ cup (⅓ pt) rum
2 cups (1 pt) chicken stock
½ cup (4 oz) brown sugar
4 tbsp of lime or lemon juice
1 tbsp flour

Score the fatty side of the pork in a criss-cross pattern. Mix the salt, pepper, cloves, ginger and garlic and rub over the scored surface. Sprinkle the crumbled bay leaves on top. Put the roast on a rack in a roasting pan with half the rum and ½ cup (¼ pt) of the stock. Roast at 325°F, 160°C, GM 3 allowing 30 minutes per pound. Half way through cooking baste the pork with a sauce made from combining the brown sugar, lime or lemon juice and the remaining rum. Add more stock to the pan during cooking if necessary. When the roast is cooked remove the bay leaves, place it on a carving board and keep hot. Spoon off the excess fat from the juices in the roasting pan and measure the remaining liquid. Make it up to 1½ cups (¾ pt) by adding more of the stock and bring it to the boil. Smooth the flour with a little water and add it to the pan, stirring constantly until the gravy has thickened. Adjust the seasoning, sieve the gravy and serve it to accompany the roast. Serves 10.

Did you know that .....
Plantains look like large bananas but are only eaten cooked. They are ripe when their skins blacken and they feel soft. A fig looks like a dumpier version of a banana. Figs taste a little like apples and are best eaten when thoroughly ripe; their skins turn yellow and they feel soft.

Fig

Banana

Monkeys are found
in St. Kitts
and Barbados

Plantain

57

Pepperpot

1 lb oxtail	1 chicken
1 calf's foot or	6 tbsp cassareep
2 pig's trotters	2-3 bonnie peppers
2 lbs lean pork or beef	Salt
½ lb salt beef	

This is a traditional dish, variations of which are found in many southern Caribbean islands. If boiled daily, it will keep and the meats can be replenished. The preserving ingredient comes from the juice of the cassava plant, used in the making of cassareep.

Joint the oxtail and quarter the calf's foot or pig's trotters. Cut the pork or beef and salt beef into 2″ cubes and the chicken into serving pieces. Put all the meat into a large casserole and cover with water. Add the cassareep and salt, and then the bonnie peppers tied in a piece of cloth. Simmer until the meats are tender and the sauce is thickened, about 1½-2 hours. Remove the peppers before serving. Serve with rice. Serves 10.

Pudding and Souse

The Pudding:

1 yard of pig's intestine	2 tbsp (1 oz) sugar
Juice of 2 limes or 1 lemon	1 tbsp flour
1 tbsp salt	2 tbsp (1 oz) margarine
2 lbs sweet potatoes	Pepper, thyme, chives and ground cloves
2 onions chopped	1 tsp hot pepper sauce

This is a traditional favourite of the English speaking Caribbean islands. Clean and wash the intestine with the salt and lime or lemon juice, then soak it for 2-3 hours. Peel and grate the sweet potatoes into a large bowl adding all the pudding ingredients. Season to taste and mix well. Lightly stuff this pudding mixture into the cleaned intestine, using a funnel. It may be easier to stuff if cut into shorter pieces. Tie the ends with string and bring to the boil, pricking a few holes in each piece to prevent splitting. Simmer until the sweet potato is cooked and the skin is firm, about 30 minutes. Serve hot, sliced into 1″ pieces.

The Souse:

2 lbs pork	1 onion chopped
1 lb cucumber diced	Parsley chopped
1 bonnie pepper seeded	Juice of 2 limes or 1 lemon
and chopped	2 tsp salt

Boil the pork for about 2 hours, until tender, and allow to cool. Dice the cucumber and put it into a large bowl with the chopped bonnie pepper and onion. (When chopping bonnie peppers hold them with a knife and fork rather than with your fingers as they will make the skin burn for about 2 hours). Add the parsley, lime or lemon juice and the salt. Mix well and add the cold pork, sliced thinly. Allow to stand for about 15 minutes before serving. Serve with slices of the "pudding" and slices of boiled breadfruit. Serves 10.

*Early Settlers catching Wild Pigs
for Pepperpot!*

Christmas Ham

4-5 lb ham	1 tsp mustard
¼ cup (2 oz) margarine	1 lb 4 oz tin crushed pineapple
Pepper	2 tbsp brown sugar
Ground nutmeg	½ cup (¼ pt) beer

Put the ham in a large saucepan, cover it with water and bring to the boil. Discard the water; this will have removed excessive salt from the ham. Melt the margarine in a roasting pan and place the ham in it. Sprinkle a little pepper and nutmeg over the top and then roast at 325°F, 160°C, GM 3 allowing 20 minutes per pound. Take the ham out of the oven and turn the oven up to 450°F, 230°C, GM 8. Put the ham onto a board, remove the skin and return the ham to the pan. Spread the mustard over the surface then cover it with as much pineapple as possible and sprinkle with the brown sugar. Put the remaining pineapple and juice into the pan with the beer. Return it to the oven for 30 minutes to melt and crisp the sugar. Serve the juices in the pan as gravy. Serves 8-10.

An alternative glaze can be made with oranges and brushed over the ham after the skin is removed. To do this dissolve ⅓ cup (3 oz) of brown sugar in ⅓ cup (4 tbsp) of orange juice and add the grated rind of 2 oranges. After brushing on this glaze use cocktail sticks to pin the orange segments to the ham. Put the remaining glazing juice into the pan. Return it to the oven for the final 30 minutes.

Lamb and Red Bean Casserole

Lamb for 6	Salt and pepper
1 cup (8 oz) dried red kidney beans	¼ tsp ground cloves
	¼ tsp thyme
2 large onions sliced	1 clove garlic crushed
1 eggplant (aubergine) cubed	4 cups (2 pts) lamb stock
¼ cup (1 oz) flour	

Soak the kidney beans overnight in water, then boil for 10 minutes and drain. Trim the fat from the meat. Melt some of it in a pan and fry the onion and eggplant for about 10 minutes, then set aside. Cut the meat into large sections, sprinkle it with the seasoned flour and brown it on all sides in the same pan. Place the lamb in a large casserole dish. Put the kidney beans amongst the lamb with the onion and eggplant on top. Season with the cloves, thyme and garlic. Cover with about 4 cups (2 pts) of stock. Bake covered, at 325°F, 160°C, GM 3 for 1½-2 hours until the beans are tender. Serves 6.

This casserole can be turned into a pie by topping it with pastry made with 2 cups (8 oz) of flour. Roll the pastry until just under ¼" thick. Moisten the edge of the pastry and press it to the edge of the casserole dish, using a central support if necessary. Make slits in the top to allow the steam to escape, decorate with cut out pastry shapes and brush with egg yolk or milk to glaze it. Bake in the same way. Serves 6.

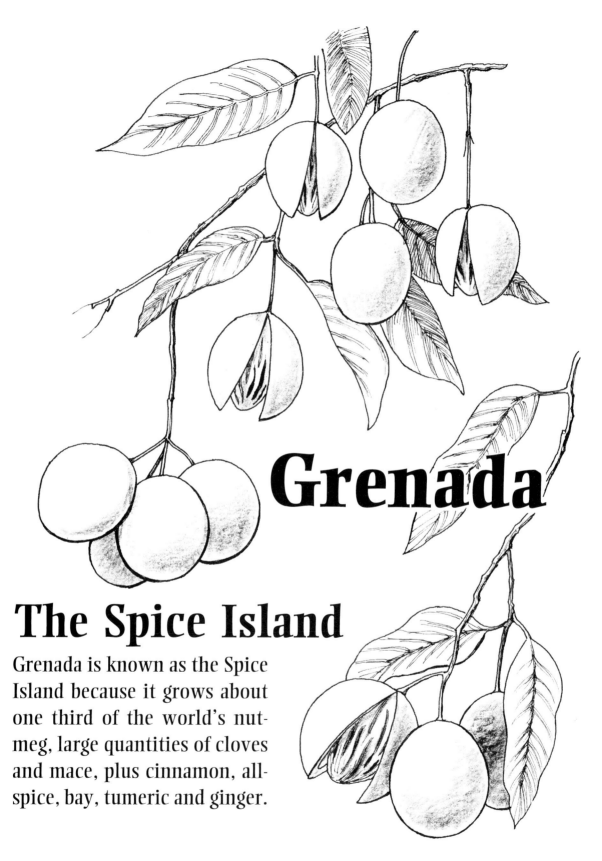

Grenada

The Spice Island

Grenada is known as the Spice Island because it grows about one third of the world's nutmeg, large quantities of cloves and mace, plus cinnamon, allspice, bay, tumeric and ginger.

Caribbean Kebabs

Steak or chicken for 6
1 lb 4 oz tin pineapple chunks
3 tbsp distilled vinegar
3 tbsp molasses
Salt and pepper
4-5 ripe plantains or bananas

2 paw-paws (papayas)
10 slices bacon
6 small tomatoes
6 small onions
Tin of 36 cocktail sausages

Mix ⅔ cup (⅓ pt) of the pineapple juice with the vinegar, molasses, salt and pepper to make a marinade. Cut the meat into 1″ cubes and marinate for at least 1 hour. Cut the plantains or bananas and the paw-paws into 1″ pieces and cut each bacon slice into 3. Quarter the tomatoes and onions. The cocktail sausages and pineapple chunks are already the right size. These ingredients can be varied to suit what is available. Thread all the ingredients alternately on 12″-18″ skewers and cook over a barbeque or under the grill for 10-15 minutes until the meat is tender and the fruit and vegetables soft and browning. Turn the kebabs and brush with the marinade every few minutes. Serve with rice. Serves 6.

Bridgetown Patties

Pastry, using 4 cups (1 lb) flour
2 tbsp cooking oil
1 lb minced beef
1 medium onion finely chopped
1 clove garlic crushed
3 tomatoes finely chopped

Salt and pepper
1 bonnie pepper seeded and chopped
  or hot pepper sauce to taste
½ tsp thyme
2 eggs beaten
1 egg white

Brown the minced beef in the oil, then add the onion and garlic and cook for 5 minutes. Add the tomato, salt, pepper, bonnie pepper or hot pepper sauce and thyme and cook for a further 5 minutes, stirring occasionally. (When chopping bonnie peppers hold them with a knife and fork rather than with your fingers as they cause the skin to burn for about 2 hours). Stir in the beaten eggs, cook for another 2-3 minutes and then allow the mixture to cool. Roll out the pastry until ⅛″ thick and cut into 5″ circles. Put about 3 tablespoonfuls of the meat mixture onto one half of each circle, then fold each over and seal the edges with a little water and press them together with a fork. Make 2 or 3 little holes in the top to allow the steam to escape and brush with the beaten egg white. Bake on an ungreased baking tray at 425°F, 220°C, GM 7 for 20-25 minutes. This makes 12 patties and serves 6. Patties also make a tasty accompaniment to drinks, in which case cut the pastry into 2″ circles, fill each with 1 teaspoonful of meat and bake for 15-20 minutes.

Did you know that .....
Paw-paw, also called papaya, is native to tropical America. It is a natural meat tenderizer from which papain is extracted for commercial use. Meat can be tenderized by wrapping it in paw-paw leaves for 1-2 hours. Like pineapple, paw-paw prevents gelatine from setting.

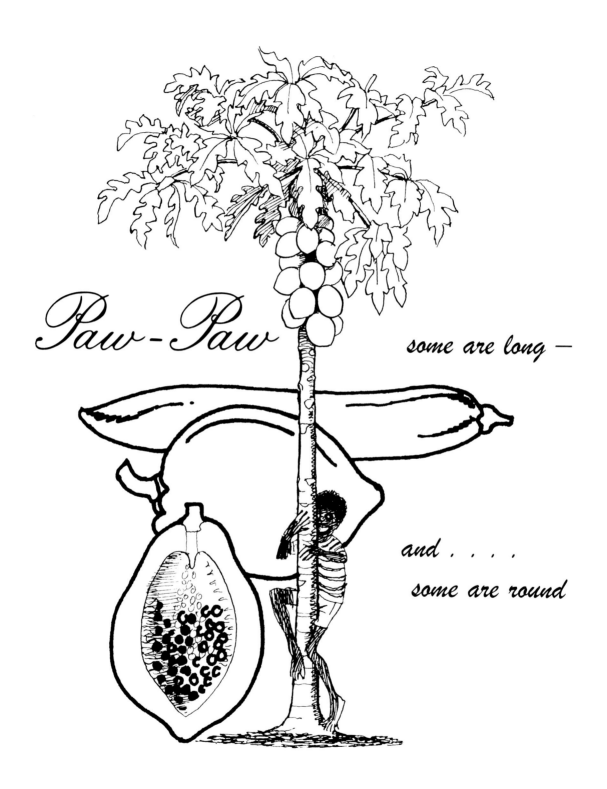

Paw-Paw

some are long —

and . . . .

some are round

Orange Roast Lamb

4 lb leg of lamb
1 clove garlic
1 tbsp cooking oil
¼ cup (1 oz) flour

Salt and pepper
½ cup (¼ pt) orange juice
3 tbsp (1½ oz) brown sugar
1 orange segmented

Make small cuts in the lamb and insert slithers of garlic. Brush the skin with the oil and dust with the seasoned flour. Roast at 350°F, 180°C, GM 4 allowing 25-30 minutes per pound. When the lamb is half cooked pour half the orange juice over it and add the remaining orange juice 10 minutes later. 10 minutes before the lamb is finished cooking sprinkle it with the brown sugar. Garnish with the orange segments. Serves 8.

Lamb and Sweet Pepper Casserole

8 lamb chops
½ cup (4 oz) black eye peas
¼ cup (2 oz) margarine
1 tsp cooking oil
4 medium onions chopped

3 medium green peppers chopped
8 oz tin tomatoes
Salt and pepper
Pinch of marjoram
1 chicken stock cube

Soak the black eye peas overnight and then cook them for 30 minutes. Cook the chops under a hot grill for 5 minutes turning once. To make the sauce, fry the onion in the margarine and oil until soft then add the green pepper and cook for 5 more minutes. Add the tomatoes, salt, pepper, marjoram and then the stock cube dissolved in ½ cup (¼ pt) of boiling water. Arrange the black eye peas around the chops in a baking dish, pour over the sauce and bake at 350°F, 180°C, GM 4 for 40 minutes. Serves 4.

Beef and Eggplant Loaf

2 medium eggplants (aubergines)
1 lb minced beef
½ lb sausage meat
1 medium onion grated
½ tsp mixed herbs

1 tbsp Worcestershire sauce
2 tbsp fresh breadcrumbs
Salt and pepper
1 egg beaten
Salad to garnish

Prick the skin of the eggplants with a fork and bake them at 375°F, 190°C, GM 5 for 30-35 minutes until softened. Cool them under running water then peel them and liquidise or chop them finely. Mix the eggplant with all the remaining ingredients and pack into a lightly greased loaf tin. Bake at 350°F, 180°C, GM 4 for 1¼-1½ hours. Serve chilled, turned out onto a serving dish and garnished with colourful salad. Serves 6-8.

Did you know that .....
The name Tobago comes from the word "tobacco" which the Carib Indians used to grow there.

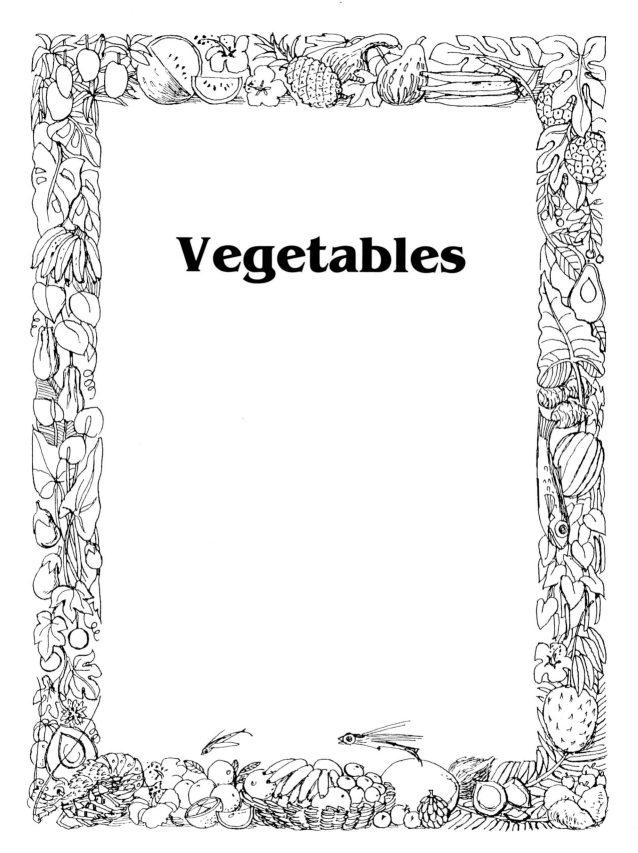

Vegetables

Rice and Peas

1⅓ cups (8 oz) rice
1 cup (½ pt) fresh pigeon peas
  or ½ cup (¼ pt) dried peas
1 tbsp vegetable oil
1 onion finely chopped
1 clove garlic crushed
½ tsp thyme
1 tbsp chopped parsley
Salt and pepper

Soak dried peas overnight, then cook until just tender, as instructed on the packet. If using fresh pigeon peas cook them in unsalted water until just tender, and then drain them. Fry the onion and garlic in the oil until lightly browned and add all the remaining ingredients except the rice. Cover and cook for 10 minutes. Meanwhile cook the rice in plenty of boiling salted water. When cooked, drain it well and stir it into the peas. Serves 4-6.

Spinach Soufflé

1 lb raw spinach
1 cup (½ pt) white sauce
Salt and pepper
2 eggs beaten

This soufflé makes an interesting dinner party dish as it is an eye-catching emerald green. Boil the spinach in salted water for 5 minutes and allow it to cool a little. Make the sauce, season it, and allow it to cool a bit too. Blend them both together in a liquidiser. Beat the eggs and gently stir them into the mixture in the liquidiser. Pour into a well greased soufflé dish and then set the dish in a shallow container of water. Bake at 350°F, 180°C, GM 4 for about 50 minutes, until risen. If the soufflé is cooked until firm it can be turned out when hot to be served cold. If baked in a ring tin the centre can be filled with a cold dish like Flying Fish Pâté or a hot dish like Lobster Casserole. Serves 6.

Oiled Down

1½ cups (8 oz) salt beef,
  pork or fish
1 cup (½ pt) coconut milk
½ a medium breadfruit
1 onion finely sliced
½ tsp thyme
Pepper
4 callaloo leaves, chinese cabbage
  or swiss chard
¼ tsp turmeric, saffron or
  curry powder (optional)

Soak the salt meat or fish for at least 8 hours. Peel the breadfruit and cut it into ¾" thick slices. Cut the salt meat into small chunks or flake the fish. Layer the breadfruit, onion and meat or fish in a heavy casserole pot. Season with the thyme and pepper, then top with the callaloo leaves. Pour the coconut milk into the casserole pot, first adding the tumeric, saffron, or curry powder to the milk if desired. To see how to extract coconut milk from a coconut, see the Coconut Crisps recipe on page 10. Much more milk is found in unripe, green coconuts. Cover and simmer gently until the breadfruit is soft, about 40-60 minutes. Delicious served with fried plantain and black eye peas. Serves 4.

GOATS
wander
in the market

67

Pumpkin Curry

2 cups (1 lb) cubed pumpkin
2 tbsp vegetable oil
1 tbsp margarine
1 onion chopped
1 green pepper chopped

4 slices bacon chopped
2 tsp curry powder
8 oz tin tomato sauce
Salt and pepper
1 clove garlic crushed

Fry the onion, green pepper and bacon in the oil and margarine for about 5 minutes. Add the curry powder and cook for a further minute or two. Add the pumpkin in ½" cubes, along with the tomato sauce, salt and pepper. Cover and simmer very gently for 20-30 minutes until the pumpkin is very soft and just starts to disintegrate. Stir occasionally to make sure that the pumpkin is not sticking and add a little water if necessary. Stir in the crushed garlic a few minutes before serving. Serves 6.

Pumpkin and Prawn "Lily"

1 small round pumpkin
1½ cups (6 oz) peeled prawns
½ cup (¼ pt) white sauce
Salt and pepper

1 blade chives chopped
1 tbsp chopped parsley
½ tsp chopped thyme
Parmesan cheese

Cut the pumpkin in half and scoop out the seeds. Cook lightly, unpeeled, for 15-20 minutes. When it is cool enough to handle, scoop out most of the flesh and chop it finely, leaving the shell ½" thick. Cut a decorative scallop round the edge of each shell. Make up the white sauce and add the prawns, chopped pumpkin and seasoning. Fill the pumpkin shells with the prawn mixture and sprinkle with parmesan. Bake at 425°F, 220°C, GM 7 for 30 minutes. Garnish each pumpkin "lily" with a prawn and some parsley. Serves 2.

Candied Sweet Potatoes

Sweet potatoes for 6
¾ cup (6 oz) brown sugar
2 tbsp butter
½ cup (¼ pt) water

1 tsp salt
1 tsp Angostura bitters
1 tsp rum

Boil the sweet potatoes in their skins for 20-30 minutes according to their size. Cool them a little then peel and slice into ¼" slices and arrange them in a lightly greased baking dish. Mix the sugar, butter, water and salt in a small pan and cook for 3 minutes over a low heat. Stir in the bitters and the rum, pour over the sweet potatoes and bake at 350°F, 180°C, GM 4 for 30 minutes. Serves 6.

Did you know that .....
Pumpkin vines are a gardener's friend as they grow best over weedy ground!

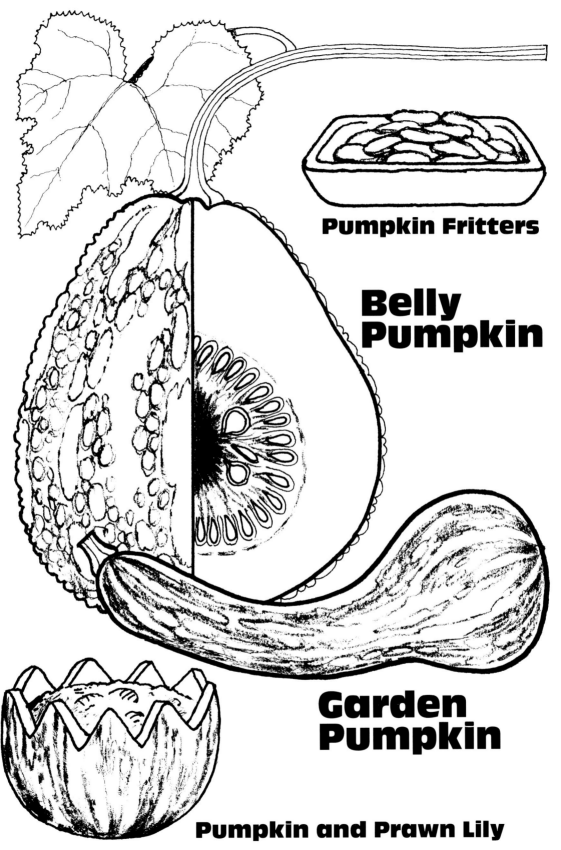

Pumpkin Fritters

Belly Pumpkin

Garden Pumpkin

Pumpkin and Prawn Lily

Tropical Fruit Curry

2 tbsp margarine
1 onion finely sliced
4 bananas sliced
3 slices pineapple cubed
1 green pepper sliced
2 large apples, peeled
  and sliced
1 tbsp curry powder

1 tbsp flour
1½ cups (¾ pt) water
6 dates chopped
2 tbsp sultanas
Juice of 1 lime or ½ a lemon
1 tsp sugar
Salt and pepper

Heat the margarine and fry the onion gently for 5 minutes, then add the banana, pineapple, green pepper and apple, and cook for a further 4·5 minutes, stirring once or twice. Mix the curry powder and flour and add it to the pan and cook for a further 2 minutes. Stir in the water, dates and sultanas and simmer for 10 minutes. Add the remaining ingredients, stirring them in very carefully to ensure the fruit is not broken. Serve immediately while the fruit is still firm, accompanied by rice. Serves 4.

Cheesy Breadfruit Croquettes

½ a medium breadfruit
1 tsp butter
1 cup (4 oz) grated cheese
Salt and pepper

1 egg beaten
Brown breadcrumbs
Oil for deep frying

Peel and cut the breadfruit into small pieces. Cook these in boiling water for about 15·20 minutes until tender. Strain and mash the breadfruit, adding the butter, cheese, salt and pepper. Mould into small croquettes, adding a few breadcrumbs if the mixture is sticky. Beat the egg with a fork adding 1 tablespoonful of water to it. Roll each croquette in dried breadcrumbs, then in the beaten egg mix and then in the breadcrumbs again. Fry them in the oil until crispy and golden brown, and drain on absorbent paper. Serves 6.

Stuffed Butternut Squash

2 butternut squash, 6″ long
8 pitted prunes finely chopped
⅓ cup (2 oz) raisins
2 tbsp rum

½ a small apple, peeled and
  finely chopped
½ a small onion finely chopped
Salt and Pepper

Butternut squash are pear-shaped, cream coloured on the outside and bright orange inside. Half a 6″ squash will be enough for one person. Soak the finely chopped prunes and raisins in the rum for about 2 hours. Then add all the remaining ingredients and mix well. Cut the unpeeled butternut squash in half lengthways, scoop out the seeds and parboil the squash for 10 minutes. Drain, and when cool enough to handle, fill with the stuffing. Bake at 350°F, 180°C, GM 4 for 35 minutes until the squash is tender. Serves 4.

Coconut Seller with Box Cart

71

Okra Ratatouille

2 medium onions chopped
1 clove garlic crushed
Cooking oil
6 okras sliced crossways
3 medium green peppers
  chopped
2 medium eggplants (aubergines)
  cubed
14½ oz tin tomatoes
1 tsp oregano
Salt and pepper

Fry the onion and garlic in just enough oil to cover the bottom of the pan. When they are soft add all the other ingredients and salt and pepper to taste. Cover and simmer gently for about 30 minutes until the vegetables are tender. Stir occasionally to prevent sticking and adjust the seasoning before serving. Serves 6.

Stuffed Eggplant

4 medium eggplants (aubergines)
Salt and pepper
1 tbsp margarine
1 large onion chopped
1 clove garlic crushed
1½ cups (¾ pt) cooked rice
1½ cups (¾ pt) stock
½ cup (¼ pt) wine or beer
Grated cheese

Halve the eggplants lengthways and score the flesh deeply with a knife. Sprinkle the flesh side with salt and pepper and then turn the halves upside down on a draining board for 30 minutes to allow the juices to drain. Carefully cut the eggplant out of the shells and chop it roughly. Melt the margarine and add the eggplant, onion, garlic, rice, stock and wine or beer. Simmer for about 20 minutes until the eggplant is tender and the liquid much reduced. Fill the eggplant shells, sprinkle the tops with grated cheese and grill until browned. Serves 4-8.

Pumpkin Fritters

2 cups (1 lb) chopped pumpkin
2 eggs beaten
1 tbsp sugar
Pinch of cinnamon
Salt and pepper
2 tsp baking powder
Flour
Lard for frying

Peel, chop and cook the pumpkin until soft, about 15-20 minutes, and then mash it. Add the beaten eggs, sugar, cinnamon, salt, pepper and baking powder and beat well. Gradually add enough sieved flour to form a thick batter consistency. Heat the lard using enough for the melted fat to be ⅛″ deep. Drop spoonfuls of the batter into the hot fat and fry both sides until golden brown, then drain on absorbent paper. Frying pumpkin fritters in lard gives a better, crisper result than using either oil or margarine. Serves 6-8.

Eggplant
(or Aubergine)

**Bonnie peppers
and Chilli peppers**

are both very very

HOT !

Greenpepper

Okras
(or Ladies' Fingers or Gumbo)

Christmas Jug

1½ cups (8 oz) chopped
   salt beef or fresh beef
2 cups (1 pt) pigeon peas
   or green peas
1 cup (4 oz) guinea corn

2 onions grated
Black pepper
Thyme
Parsley chopped
1 tbsp butter

This is a favourite Barbadian Christmas dish, often known as "jug jug". If using the traditional choice of salt beef it needs to be soaked overnight to reduce its saltiness. Trim off any fat and cut the meat into small pieces. Put the meat and peas into a pan, cover with water and cook for 20-30 minutes. If using frozen green peas add these only for the last 10 minutes as they will cook faster. Drain the water but retain it. Lightly liquidise the beef and peas. Put the guinea corn into the pan and cover it with some of the water used to cook the meat. Cook for 5 minutes keeping it stirred and smooth. Add the meat and peas, onion, pepper, thyme, parsley and butter. Cook over a very low heat for about 30 minutes. Adjust the seasoning, particularly adding salt if fresh beef was used, and serve with a little butter on top. Serves 8-10.

Coo Coo

12 small, young okras
2½ pints water
salt to taste

8 oz. yellow cornmeal
1½ oz. unsalted butter

Slice the okras cross wise 1/4" thick. Add salt and okras to boiling water and boil covered for ten minutes. Pour the cornmeal into the water in a slow steady stream, stirring with a wooden spoon. Stir constantly over a medium heat until the mixture is thick and smooth. Mould in a greased basin for five minutes. Then turn out onto a warm dish and spread the butter on top. Serve hot - serves 6.

Christophene Cheese

6 small christophenes
2 cups (1 pt) white sauce
Parsley chopped

Salt and pepper
Grated cheese
Breadcrumbs

Christophenes, when peeled, leave a sticky residue on your hands. To avoid this rub your hands lightly with oil beforehand. Peel the christophenes and cut them lengthways into quarters, discarding the cores. Boil for 15-20 minutes then place in a shallow baking dish. Season the white sauce with parsley, salt and pepper and pour it over the christophenes. Sprinkle with a few tablespoonfuls of breadcrumbs and the grated cheese. Place under the grill until the top is crisp and golden brown, about 10 minutes. Serves 6.

Did you know that .....
Early Scottish settlers made "jug" as a substitute for their traditional Scottish dish Haggis.

The country bus loads up . . . . . !

Yam Soufflé

Yams for 6
⅓ cup (3 oz) butter
¾ cup (⅓ pt) milk

1 cup (4 oz) grated cheese
Salt and pepper
3 eggs separated

Peel, chop and cook the yam until soft, about 20 minutes, and then mash it. Melt the butter in the milk in a large pan, then add the mashed yam, half the cheese, and the salt and pepper. Mix well then remove from the heat. Fold in the beaten egg yolks and then fold in the stiffly beaten egg whites quite gently. Put in a lightly greased baking dish and sprinkle with the remaining grated cheese. Bake at 350°F, 180°C, GM 4 for 30 minutes until browned. Sweet potatoes make a nice alternative soufflé if substituted for the yams. Serves 6.

Plantains in Bacon

4 ripe plantains

12 slices streaky bacon

Plantains are ripe when their skins begin to blacken and they feel soft. The combined flavours of sweet plantain and savoury bacon is delicious. Peel the plantains and slice each into 6 chunks. Halve the bacon slices and wrap a piece around each chunk of plantain, securing with a cocktail stick. Stand each on its end in a baking dish and bake at 350°F, 180°C, GM 4 for about 40 minutes until the bacon is crispy and the plantain soft. These are very quick to prepare and are ideal for baking around roasts. Serves 6-8.

Conkies

½ cup (2 oz) flour
1 small sweet potato grated
1 small coconut grated
2 cups (1 lb) grated pumpkin
2 cups (8 oz) rough corn meal
½-1 tsp mixed essence
1 tsp mixed spice
1 tsp ground nutmeg

Pinch of salt
1 cup (8 oz) sugar
½ cup (4 oz) margarine
¼ cup (2 oz) shortening
Up to 1 cup (½ pt milk)
For wrapping: Banana leaves
   or grease proof paper

This is a traditional Barbadian dish. To see how to prepare a coconut for grating turn to the Coconut Crisps recipe on page 10. Combine all the ingredients except the fats and milk. Mix well and then add the melted margarine and shortening. Mix to a smooth paste. If the mixture is too dry add up to 1 cup (½ pt) of milk. Cut the spine out of the banana leaves and cut the pieces on either side into about twelve 8″ squares. If you do not happen to have banana leaves to hand, squares of grease proof paper are the best substitute. Put about 2 tablespoonfuls of the mixture onto each square and fold each into a parcel securing with a cocktail stick or thread. Steam over boiling water for ¾-1 hour. Serves 4-6.

Root Vegetables

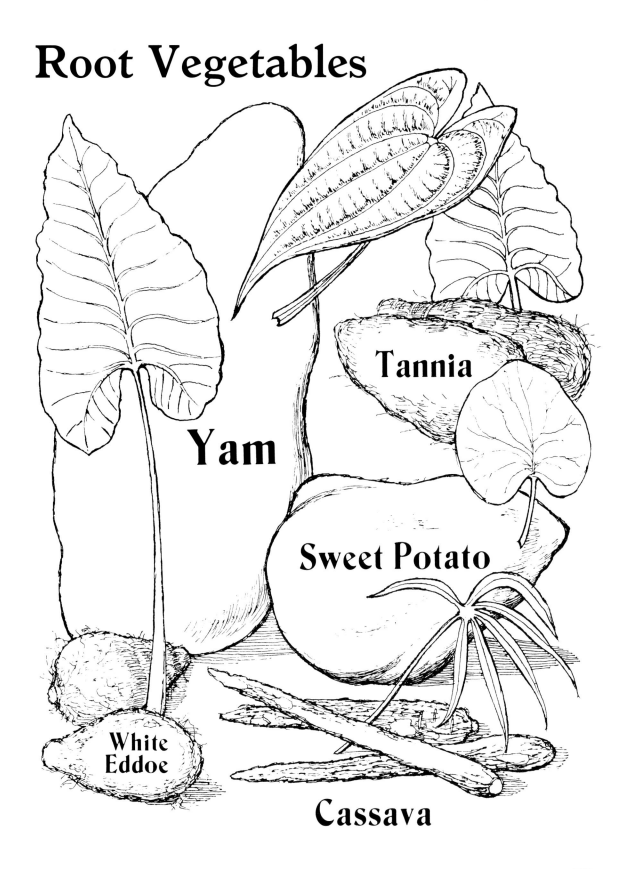

Tannia

Yam

Sweet Potato

White
Eddoe

Cassava

77

Spinach and Cottage Cheese Quiche

9″ pie shell unbaked,
  using 1½ cups (6 oz) flour
½ lb spinach, fresh or frozen
1 cup (8 oz) cottage cheese
2 eggs

4 tbsp evaporated milk
1 clove garlic crushed
Salt and pepper
½ cup (2 oz) parmesan cheese

First make the pie shell ready. Then cook the spinach lightly, chopping it first if using fresh spinach. Drain well and allow to cool. Beat together the cottage cheese, eggs and the evaporated milk. Add the garlic, salt and pepper and then stir in the spinach. Pour into the pie shell and sprinkle with parmesan cheese. Bake at 350°F, 180°C, GM 4 for 30-35 minutes. Serves 6.

Sweet Potato Soufflé

2 cups (1 pt) cooked and
  mashed sweet potato
2 eggs separated

¼ tsp ground nutmeg
½ tsp ground ginger
1 cup (½ pt) milk

Separate the egg yolks and whites and mix the yolks thoroughly with all the other ingredients. Whisk the egg whites until stiff and fold them gently into the sweet potato mixture. Turn it into a lightly greased baking dish and bake at 350°F, 180°C, GM 4 for about 45 minutes, until browned on top and well risen. Serves 4-6.

Sweet Corn Fritters

1 egg
3 tbsp milk
3 tbsp natural yoghurt
1 cup (4 oz) self raising flour

Salt and pepper
7 oz tin sweet corn
Oil for frying

Put the egg, milk, yoghurt, flour and salt in a blender and blend until smooth. Drain the sweet corn and stir it into the batter. Heat the oil, then drop large spoonfuls of the fritter mixture into the hot oil. Fry each side until golden brown, about two minutes each side, then drain on absorbent paper. Makes about 12 fritters. Serves 6.

Did you know that .....
The Dutch Antilles consist of two groups of islands. These are Aruba, Bonaire and Curaçao off the coast of Venezuela and St Eustatius, Saba and St Maarten, all further north. The first group are known as the "ABC's" and the second group as the "3 S's". St Maarten is in fact only part of an island, the other part, St Martin, is French.

Digging Sweet Potatoes

Sweet Potato Pie

11" pie shell unbaked,
   using 2 cups (8 oz) flour
¾ cup (6 oz) margarine
¾ cup (6 oz) sugar
1½ cups (¾ pt) grated
   sweet potato
⅓ cup (4 tbsp) milk
¾ tsp ground ginger
Grated rind of 2 oranges
1 tbsp orange juice
A little salt

Prick the base of the unbaked pie shell thoroughly and bake for 10 minutes at 400°F, 200°C, GM 6. Allow to cool. Cream the margarine and sugar until light and fluffy. Gradually add the sweet potato, milk, ginger, orange rind, juice and salt, and beat well. Pour into the pie shell and bake at 300°F, 150°C, GM 2 for about 45 minutes until lightly browned. This pie is very rich and will serve 10.

Eggplant Casserole

4 slices streaky bacon
3 small onions chopped
3 medium green peppers
   chopped
1 large eggplant (aubergine)
   cubed
2 tsp salt
¼ tsp black pepper
8 oz tin tomatoes
Grated cheese
1½ cups (1½ oz) cornflakes
   crushed

Fry the bacon until crispy and then set aside to use later. Fry the onion and green pepper in the bacon fat for 5 minutes. Peel and cube the eggplant and add it to the pan with the salt, pepper, tomatoes and 1 cup (½ pt) of water. Cover and cook for 10 minutes until the eggplant is nearly tender. Pour into a shallow casserole dish and sprinkle with the grated cheese, cornflake crumbs and crumbled bacon. Bake uncovered at 350°F, 180°C, GM 4 for 20-30 minutes. Serves 4.

Baked Stuffed Paw-Paw

1 large green paw-paw (papaya),
   about 8"-9" long
2 tbsp (1 oz) margarine
1 large onion chopped
2 medium tomatoes chopped
Salt and pepper
1½ cups (3 oz) bread crumbs
½ cup (2 oz) finely grated
   parmesan or cheddar cheese

Paw-paw is usually eaten as a fruit, but when green and unripe it is used as a vegetable. Halve the unpeeled paw-paw lengthways and remove the seeds. Cook the halves in salted water for 15-20 minutes until tender. Drain, then scoop out and mash the flesh, carefully keeping the skins intact. Fry the onion in the margarine until soft, stir in the tomatoes, salt, pepper and mashed paw-paw. Fill the paw-paw shells with the stuffing, sprinkle with the breadcrumbs and cheese. Bake at 400°F, 200°C, GM 6 until browned. Serves 6.

Desserts

Latticed Mango Pie

9" pie shell unbaked with
enough pastry for lattice
using 2¼ cups (9 oz) flour
⅓ cup (3 oz) sugar
¼ tsp ground cinnamon

¼ tsp ground nutmeg
5 cups (2½ pts) sliced fresh mango
1 tsp lime or lemon juice
1 tbsp milk

This is a dessert from Grenada, but in all the islands when the mango season comes you need as many mango recipes as possible to cope with so much fruit! First make the pie shell ready. Then put the sugar, cinnamon, nutmeg, sliced mango and lime or lemon juice in a bowl and mix well. Tip the mixture into the pie shell and make it level. To make the decorative lattice top, roll out the remaining pastry into a rectangle 10" long. Slice this into 10-12 strips of ¼" wide and lay them in a lattice pattern over the mango filling, trimming them to fit. Where the lattice strips meet the pie shell around the edges, join them by dotting with a little water and pressing them to seal. Brush the lattice with the milk to glaze, then bake at 400°F, 200°C, GM 6 for 50 minutes. Serves 6-8.

Rum and Coffee Cream

1 tbsp unflavoured gelatine
1½ cups (¾ pt) milk
½ cup (4 oz) castor sugar
2 egg yolks beaten
1½ tsp custard powder

A little milk
1 tsp coffee essence
1 tbsp rum
½ cup (¼ pt) evaporated milk
A little grated dark chocolate

Combine the gelatine, milk and sugar in a pan and let stand for 5 minutes to soften the gelatine. Stir over a low heat until the gelatine is dissolved, about 7 minutes. Stir in the beaten egg yolks and continue stirring over a medium heat for 5 minutes. Mix the custard powder smoothly with a little milk and stir it into the gelatine mixture, stirring until the custard thickens and coats the back of the spoon, about 5 minutes. Remove from the heat and cool. Add the rum and coffee essence, then beat the evaporated milk until it is frothy and fold it in too. Pour into a serving dish, place in the freezer for 15 minutes and then transfer to the fridge, chilling for at least 30 minutes. Decorate with a little grated chocolate before serving. Mini versions of either Coconut Pitons or Coconut Meringues make a nice accompaniment to this light and creamy dessert. Serves 6.

Did you know that .....
Mango trees are usually grafted to allow selection of the sweetest and least stringy fruits. Favourite varieties include the Julie, Bombay, Ceylon, Dr Roland, Parwee, Graham, Haden, Kitt, Kent, Alphonse, Palmer, Edward and Peter. The smallest is "Thousand", typically 4 oz, and the largest is "Sensation" which can weigh an amazing 4 lbs!

TO PREPARE A MANGO

Hold the fruit upright and cut down either side of the stone. Now score the flesh of each side in a criss-cross pattern and then scoop it out. These will be neat bite-size pieces. Next cut the strip of skin from around the central section containing the stone and cut away the remaining fruit.

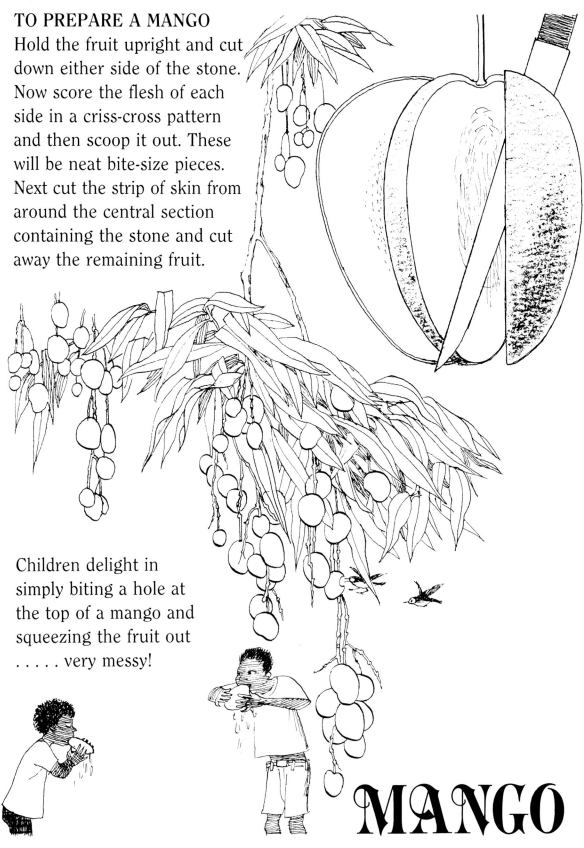

Children delight in simply biting a hole at the top of a mango and squeezing the fruit out . . . . . very messy!

MANGO

Guava Tart

9″ pie shell unbaked,
  using 1½ cups (6 oz) flour
About 20 fresh guavas, or
  a large tin of guavas
1 cup (8 oz) brown sugar

¼ cup (1 oz) cornflour
1 tsp vanilla essence
1 tbsp butter
Grated coconut

Prick the base of the unbaked pie shell thoroughly. Cover with a piece of grease proof paper and fill with rice. Bake at 400°F, 200°C, GM 6 for 10 minutes, then remove the rice and paper and bake for a further 10 minutes. Allow to cool. If using fresh guavas, peel off their fine skin, halve them and scoop out and reserve the seeds. Simmer the guava shells in 1¼ cups (⅔ pt) of water for 10-15 minutes until they are soft. When cool arrange decoratively in the pie shell. To make the glaze add the seeds and sugar to the water that the guavas were cooked in and simmer for 5 minutes. Sieve the juice and return it to the pan. Mix the cornflour smoothly with a little of the juice and add it to the pan. Add the vanilla and simmer, stirring for 5 minutes until thickened. Stir in the butter and pour the glaze over the guavas. If using tinned guavas, use the reserved juice to make the glaze, topping it up with water. Serve chilled, sprinkled with grated coconut. Serves 6-8.

Coconut Meringue Pie

9″ pie shell unbaked,
  using 1½ cups (6 oz) flour
1 cup (½ pt) milk
1 cup (3 oz) grated coconut

¼ cup (2 oz) castor sugar
A little ground nutmeg
1 tsp vanilla essence
3 egg yolks beaten

Meringue:
3 egg whites
½ cup (4 oz) castor sugar

Vanilla essence

To see how to prepare a coconut for grating turn to the Coconut Crisps recipe on page 10. Prick the base of the unbaked pie shell thoroughly and bake for 10 minutes at 400°F, 200°C, GM 6. Allow to cool. Heat the milk and stir in all the ingredients of the filling. Pour the mixture into the pie shell and bake at 450°F, 230°C, GM 8 for 10 minutes. Reduce the temperature to 375°F, 190°C, GM 5 and bake for a further 35 minutes until the filling has set. Allow to cool and then make the meringue.

Meringue: Beat the egg whites until stiff and then add the sugar and vanilla a little at a time. Spread the meringue over the filling, covering the pastry edge so that it will not be over browned. Return to the oven for about 12 minutes until the top of the meringue is lightly browned. Served hot or cold, this is delicious with vanilla ice cream. Serves 6-8.

Did you know that .....
A coconut is fresh if you can hear the coconut "milk" moving inside when the coconut is shaken.

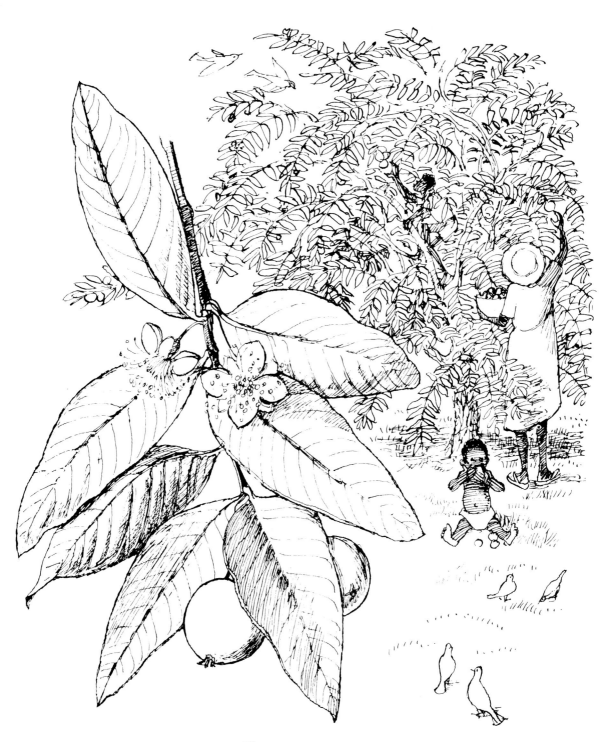

Guavas

Peanut Molasses Pie

9" pie shell unbaked,
    using 1½ cups (6 oz) flour
½ cup (¼ pt) molasses
1 tsp butter
2 eggs
½ cup (4 oz) sugar

1 tbsp flour
½ cup (¼ pt) milk
¼ tsp salt
¾ cup (3 oz) chopped peanuts,
    fresh and unsalted
½ tsp vanilla essence

Prick the base of the unbaked pie shell thoroughly and bake for 10 minutes at 400°F, 200°C, GM 6. Allow to cool. Bring the molasses and butter to the boil and then set aside. Beat the eggs and gradually beat in the sugar and flour. Stir in the milk, salt and molasses mixture. Add the nuts and vanilla and pour it all into the pie shell. Bake at 425°F, 220°C, GM 7 for 10 minutes and then reduce the temperature to 325°F, 160°C, GM 3 for 25-30 minutes until the filling has set. Serves 6-8.

Passion Fruit Cream

2 cups (1 pt) thick custard
2 tbsp (1 oz) brown sugar

5 passion fruit

Passion fruit have a most exotic flavour and as they get riper their skins get more and more wrinkled. Normally the seeds are eaten along with the pulp, but for this dish they are removed. Make the custard thick enough to hold its shape and sweeten it with the sugar. Strain the passion fruit pulp to remove the seeds and stir the juice into the custard. Serve very hot or very cold with vanilla ice cream. This simple dish is also delicious using stewed guava purée in place of the passion fruit. Serves 4.

Tropical Fruit Ice Creams

4 egg yolks
½ cup (4 oz) castor sugar

1½ cups (¾ pt) milk
½ cup (¼ pt) double cream

Beat the egg yolks and sugar. Heat the milk and cream, then pour into the egg mixture very slowly, stirring continuously. Return the mixture to the pan in which the milk and cream were heated. Cook over water, stirring continuously, for about 20 minutes until the mixture is a thick and creamy custard consistency. Allow to cool and then stir in the fruit pulp, see choice below. The volume will now be about 3½ cups (1¾ pts or 1 litre), so choose a container larger than this and pour the ice cream mixture into it. Put to freeze, but it is important to take the ice cream out and whisk it three times during the first two hours of freezing. This prevents ice crystals from forming in the ice cream. Serves 8-10.

Mango, Guava, Pineapple or Soursop: 1½ cups (¾ pt) purée with 3-4 tbsp sugar.
Banana ice cream: 3 ripe bananas, mashed.
Rum and Raisin ice cream: 1 cup (5 oz) raisins chopped, soaked for 4 hours in 4 tbsp rum.

Peanut Vendors

87

Pineapple Pie

9″ pie shell unbaked, and
  pastry to cover, using
  2½ cups (10 oz) flour
1 large pineapple chopped
1 cup (8 oz) sugar

¼ cup (1 oz) flour
¼ tsp ground nutmeg
Pinch of cinnamon
Pinch of salt
3 tbsp (1½ oz) butter

Prick the base of the unbaked pie shell thoroughly and bake for 10 minutes at 400°F, 200°C, GM 6. Allow to cool. Mix the pineapple, sugar, flour, nutmeg, cinnamon and salt and stir over a low heat until the mixture thickens. Remove from the heat and stir in the butter and if necessary add a little water to achieve a soft creamy consistency around the pineapple. Allow to cool. Pour the mixture into the pie shell and cover with a lid of thin pastry. Seal the two together around the edges with a little water and press them together with a fork. Make three little slits in the top to allow the steam to escape and decorate with pineapple shapes cut from the remaining pastry. Bake at 425°F, 220°C, GM 7 for 10 minutes then reduce the temperature to 325°F, 160°C, GM 3 for 30 minutes until the crust is lightly browned. Serves 6-8.

Coconut Caramels

½ cup plus 1 tbsp (4½ oz)
  castor sugar
1½ cups (4½ oz) grated coconut

2 cups (1 pt) milk
4 eggs beaten

Dissolve ½ cup (4 oz) of the sugar in ½ cup (¼ pt) of water over a gentle heat, and then cook without stirring until it turns a rich brown colour, about 20 minutes. Do not allow it to become too dark or it will taste slightly bitter. Quickly use it to coat the inside of 4 individual serving bowls. Pour it from one bowl to another holding the bowl in a cloth as it will become hot when the caramel is poured in. Leave to set. Add most of the coconut to the milk and bring to the boil, then set aside for 20 minutes. Squeeze the milk from the coconut and discard the dry coconut. Reheat the milk but do not allow it to boil. Stir it into the beaten eggs and the remaining 1 tablespoonful (½ oz) of sugar. Strain the mixture into the prepared bowls and then set the bowls in a shallow container of cold water. Bake for about 1¼ hours at 250°F, 120°C, GM ½ until set. When cooked loosen around the top of each with a knife and turn them very gently out onto individual serving plates. Serve chilled, sprinkled with the remaining grated coconut. Serves 4.

Did you know that .....
Pineapples grow best in the volcanic Caribbean islands, like Martinique, where the soil is acid. Plants grow to 3′ high and consist of slender greyish green leaves sprouting from ground level. The flower spike grows up from the centre. It has numerous tiny flowers which each develop tightly packed separate fruits which then grow together to give the familiar pineapple!

PINEAPPLES
grow well in the volcanic soil of Martinique

Soursop Cream

3 tbsp margarine
2 tbsp cornflour
1 cup (½ pt) milk

2 tbsp honey
1½ cups (¾ pt) sieved soursop

Melt the margarine over a low heat then add the cornflour and blend it well. Remove from the heat and add the milk a little at a time, stirring well to ensure it is smooth. Stir constantly over a medium heat until the mixture thickens and comes to the boil. Allow to boil for one minute and then add the honey and set it aside to cool. Stir in the soursop purée and chill before serving. Serves 4.

Pitch Lake Pudding

2 cups (12 oz) chocolate chips
1 tbsp unflavoured gelatine
1 tbsp butter

7 eggs separated
½ tbsp vanilla essence
2 tbsp rum

Because of its dark chocolate colour this dessert is named after Trinidad's famous Pitch Lake. In 1595 Sir Walter Raleigh took pitch from the lake to caulk his ships, and today the lake still supplies asphalt.

Soak the gelatine in 3 tablespoonfuls of hot water for a few minutes. Add it to the chocolate chips and butter and heat, stirring until melted. Remove from the heat and add the lightly beaten egg yolks, vanilla and rum. Beat the egg whites until stiff. Stir half into the chocolate mixture and then fold the second half in very gently. Pour into a glass bowl and chill for several hours, putting it in the freezer for the first hour. Serves 8-10.

Rum and Raisin Soufflé

1½ tbsp cornflour
1 cup (½ pt) evaporated milk
5 eggs separated
¾ cup (6 oz) castor sugar
1½ tbsp unflavoured gelatine

1 tsp vanilla essence
8 tbsp rum
3 tbsp raisins chopped
Pinch of salt

Smooth the cornflour with 3 tablespoonfuls of water and stir with the evaporated milk over a low heat until thick, then set aside. Beat the egg yolks and sugar until thick and pale yellow. Sprinkle the gelatine onto ⅓ cup (4 tbsp) of water to soften for a few minutes then add the gelatine, the egg yolks and sugar into the cornflour mixture and stir over a gentle heat for 5 minutes. Stir in the vanilla, rum and raisins. Add the salt to the egg whites and beat until stiff. Stir half into the yolk mixture and then fold the second half in very gently. Pour into a glass bowl and chill until set. Serves 8.

For a quick and easy rum and raisin dessert, soak several tablespoonfuls of raisins in rum for a few hours or overnight and serve sprinkled over vanilla ice cream.

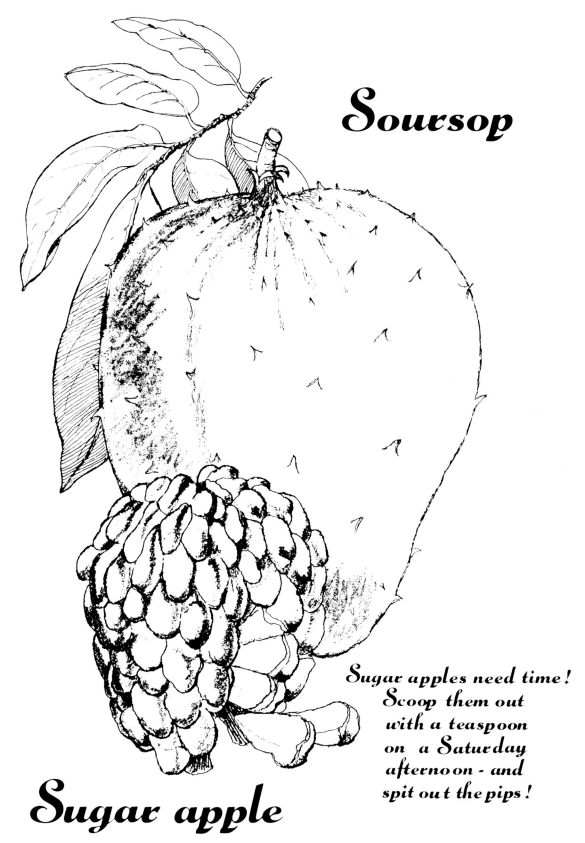

Soursop

Sugar apple

Sugar apples need time!
Scoop them out
with a teaspoon
on a Saturday
afternoon - and
spit out the pips!

Tropical Trifle

7-8" sponge cake
6 tbsp sherry or rum liqueur
Guava, cherry or mango jam
4-5 bananas sliced
1 small paw-paw (papaya) cubed

½ cup (1½ oz) grated coconut
Pineapple pieces
3 oranges segmented
2 cups (1 pt) custard
½ tsp vanilla essence

Break the cake into small pieces and place in a glass bowl. Add the sherry then cover with cling film and chill for 1-2 hours. Spread a little of the jam over the cake and then add the different layers of fruit, varying them to suit what is available - sliced bananas, paw-paw pieces, half the coconut, pineapple pieces, more banana and then the orange segments and their juice. Bring each layer of fruit to the edge of the bowl so that the colours of each can be seen. Make the custard thick and creamy and slightly less sweet than usual. Add to it the vanilla essence and most of the remaining coconut, retaining a little for decoration. Allow the custard to cool slightly before pouring it over the fruit. Chill the trifle for several hours or overnight to allow the flavours to mix and the custard to set. Decorate with fruit and grated coconut. Serves 8-10.

Golden Coconut Dessert

2 cups (1 lb) white sugar
⅔ cup (⅓ pt) water
2 cups (6 oz) grated coconut
2 egg yolks beaten
½ cup (2 oz) plain flour

¾ tsp baking powder
Pinch of salt
Grated rind of 1 lime or ½ a lemon
2½ tbsp (1¼ oz) butter
1 tbsp rum

Bring the sugar and water to the boil and allow to boil until a light syrup forms, about 10 minutes. Stir in the grated coconut and cook for a further 5 minutes, until the coconut looks cooked. Remove from the heat and allow to cool a little before stirring in the beaten egg yolks. Sieve the flour and baking powder and stir it into the coconut mixture along with the salt, lime or lemon rind, butter and rum. Pour into a lightly greased baking dish, about 12" x 7", and bake at 350°F, 180°C, GM 4 for about 35 minutes until the top is golden brown. Serves 6.

Mango Water Ice

1 cup (½ pt) mango pulp
½ cup plus 2 tbsp (5 oz)
  white sugar

Grated rind and juice of
  1 lime or ½ a lemon
1 cup (½ pt) water

Heat the sugar and the lime or lemon rind in the water and simmer for 3 minutes. Liquidise the mango and add the syrup and the lime or lemon juice. Pour into a container and put it in the freezer. When it begins to freeze around the edges, (after about two hours) take it out and whisk it, then return it to freeze fully. Makes 2 cups (1 pt). Serves 4.

TROPICAL TRIFLE

Barbados Cherry Jelly

1 cup (½ pt) cherry skins,
  juice and pulp
Sugar to sweeten cherries

1 packet raspberry, strawberry
  or blackberry jelly

During the cherry season prepared fruit can be put in the freezer to use throughout the year. Preparing the cherries is a slow process but they taste so good that it is well worthwhile. Either squeeze the seeds from each cherry individually or cut the fruit from the seeds. More pulp can be got by squeezing the seeds as well. Combine the fruit and pulp and add several heaped tablespoonfuls of sugar. Dissolve the jelly in 1½ cups (¾ pt) of hot water and add the fruit. Pour into a glass bowl and chill until set. Serves 6.

Fruit Soufflés

½ cup (¼ pt) evaporated milk
1 packet jelly, lemon or
  raspberry
1 egg separated

6-8 limes or passion fruit or 1 cup (½ pt)
  sweetened Barbados Cherry pulp or guava purée
Ice cubes

Chill the evaporated milk thoroughly. For a lime, passion fruit or guava soufflé use a lemon jelly and for a cherry soufflé use a raspberry jelly. Dissolve the jelly in 1 cup (½ pt) of hot water and make it up to 2 cups (1 pt) with the fruit juice or purée, adding a few ice cubes to top it up if necessary. Beat the egg yolk and add it to the jelly and fruit mixture and chill. When the jelly begins to set beat the evaporated milk until it is thick and frothy and mix it into the jelly. Beat the egg white until stiff and gently fold it in. Pour into a glass bowl and chill until set. Serves 8.

Hot Banana Meringue Pudding

3 medium bananas
1 cup (2 oz) fresh breadcrumbs
1 egg separated
1 cup (½ pt) milk

Peeled rind of 1 lime or ½ a lemon
¾ cup (6 oz) light brown sugar
¼ tsp ground nutmeg
1 tbsp castor sugar

Liquidise or mash the bananas and then stir in the breadcrumbs. (Liquidising is preferable to mashing the bananas as it will make the banana lighter). In a separate bowl beat the egg yolk with the milk and the lime or lemon rind. Peel the rind in large, easily seen pieces as it is removed later. Add the sugar and the nutmeg and beat until the sugar is completely dissolved. Remove the rind and then stir in the banana. Pour into a lightly greased baking dish and cook at 325°F, 160°C , GM 3 until a knife inserted in the middle comes out clean, about 30 minutes. To make the meringue beat the egg white until stiff then beat in the castor sugar. Spread the meringue over the cooked pudding and return it to the oven for a few minutes until lightly browned. Serves 4-6.

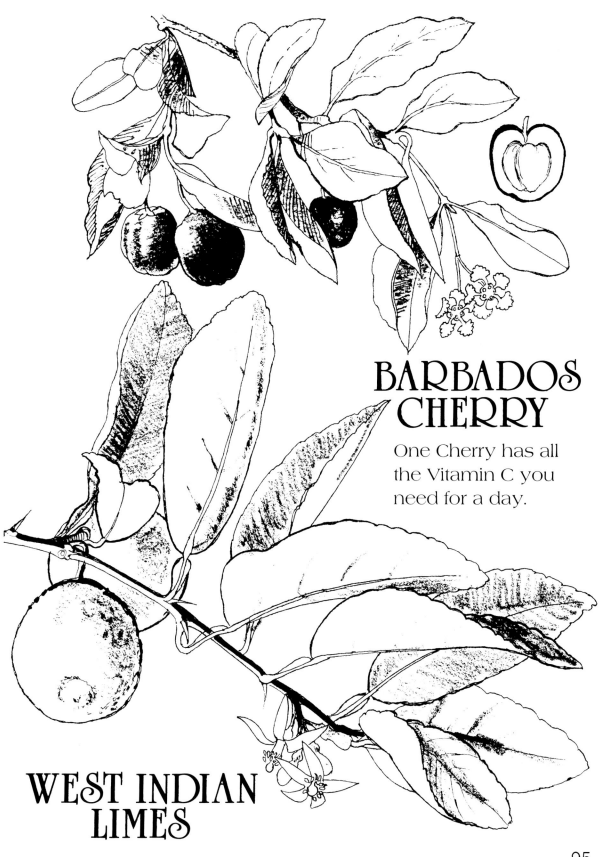

BARBADOS CHERRY

One Cherry has all
the Vitamin C you
need for a day.

WEST INDIAN LIMES

Rum and Orange Banana Flambé

6 large bananas
Grated rind of ½ an orange
Juice of 1 orange
Pinch of ground nutmeg

¼ cup (2 oz) brown sugar
¼ cup (2 oz) butter
½ cup (¼ pt) rum

Put the unpeeled bananas on a baking tray and bake at 350°F, 180°C, GM 4 for 10 minutes, turning them once and after 10 minutes the skins will have blackened. (This stage can be omitted if the bananas are well ripened as they will be soft enough). When they have cooled enough to handle, peel them, halve them lengthways and arrange in a heat-proof serving dish. In a small bowl mix the grated orange rind, orange juice and nutmeg and pour it over the bananas. Sprinkle over the sugar and dot with the butter. Place under a hot grill for about 6 minutes, until the sugar has melted and bubbles. While the bananas are grilling heat the rum gently for just two minutes. When the bananas are ready ignite the rum and pour it flaming over the bananas. Serve while still alight. Serves 6.

Variations of this recipe include grilling the bananas with only brown sugar sprinkled over them or using a few tablespoonfuls of any fruit juice and some grated coconut. Grilled bananas are delicious served with vanilla ice cream.

Spicy Pumpkin Pudding

2 eggs separated
¼ cup (2 oz) brown sugar
¾ cup (⅓ pt) pumpkin purée
1 tbsp plain flour
½ tsp ground ginger
1 tsp cinnamon
¼ tsp ground cloves

Pinch of salt
½ cup (¼ pt) evaporated milk chilled
¼ cup (3 tbsp) milk
1 tbsp molasses
Pinch of cream of tartar
1½ tbsp castor sugar

Beat the egg yolks and brown sugar until the mixture forms ribbons when the beaters are lifted. Stir in the pumpkin purée. In a small bowl mix the flour, ginger, cinnamon, cloves and salt and then stir it into the pumpkin mixture. Beat the evaporated milk until thick and frothy and add it to the pumpkin mixture along with the milk and the molasses. In a clean bowl beat the egg whites with the cream of tartar until they hold in soft peaks. Slowly add the castor sugar and continue beating until stiff. Gently fold the egg whites into the pumpkin mixture and then pour it into a 4 cup (2 pt) baking dish. Place the dish in a baking pan adding hot water to the level of 1½″ up the side of the dish. Bake at 375°F, 190°C, GM 5 for 55 minutes to 1 hour, until the pudding is risen and firm. Allow to cool for 10 minutes before serving. Serves 4-6.

Did you know that .....
Banana trees are cut down after bearing once, and a new sucker grows up to bear the next crop.

Cakes
and Cookies

Bakes

4 cups (1 lb) self raising flour
1 tbsp baking powder
1 tbsp sugar
¾ tbsp salt
¼ cup (2 oz) margarine
Oil for deep frying

Bakes are fried rolls which are traditionally made in many islands as a substitute for bread. They taste like a cross between bread and dumplings. Sieve the flour, baking powder, sugar and salt into a large mixing bowl. Add the margarine, cutting it into small pieces and then rubbing it into the flour with your finger tips. When the mixture is fine and crumbly make a well in the centre and slowly add about 1½ cups (¾ pt) of cold water, mixing it in all the time. Turn the dough onto a floured board and knead until smooth. Divide the dough into 12 pieces, roll each into a ball and then flatten them evenly until ¼" thick. Fry a few at a time in ½" of hot oil over a medium heat. Turn them several times and after about 3-5 minutes, when they are golden brown, take them out and drain on kitchen paper. Keep them hot while the remaining bakes are cooked. Serve as bread rolls with a meal or with fillings of your choice. Makes 12.

Coconut Carrot Cake

1 cup (8 oz) white sugar
1 cup (½ pt) corn or vegetable oil
3 eggs
1½ cups (6 oz) plain flour
1⅓ tsp baking powder
1 tsp bicarbonate of soda
1½ tsp ground cinnamon
¼ tsp ground nutmeg
½ tsp salt
2 cups (6 oz) grated carrot
1½ cups (4½ oz) grated coconut

Mix the sugar and the corn or vegetable oil together and add the eggs one at a time, beating well after each one. Sift the dry ingredients and add to the sugar mixture, beating to mix well. Fold in the grated carrot and grated coconut. Pour into a lightly greased round 8" cake tin which is 2" deep and bake at 300°F, 150°C, GM 2 for 55 minutes. Coconut Carrot Cake is good served hot as a dessert accompanied by ice cream and decorated with sliced banana, or cooled and served as a tea cake, with icing.

Icing: (Optional)
1 cup (8 oz) cream cheese
¼ cup (2 oz) butter
2 cups (8 oz) icing sugar
2 tsp vanilla essence

Cream the butter and cheese. Add the sifted icing sugar and the vanilla and mix until smooth. When the cake is cool spread the icing over the top.

Did you know that .....
The central shoot of a coconut palm is known as "heart of palm" and is eaten as a vegetable. However, cutting it kills the whole tree, so it is forbidden by law in many countries.

BAKES
being cooked beside the road in TRINIDAD

Coconut Cream Gâteau

¼ cup (2 oz) margarine
¼ cup (2 oz) shortening
1½ cups (12 oz) castor sugar
2½ cups (10 oz) plain flour
2½ tsp baking powder

1 tsp salt
1 cup (½ pt) milk
1 tsp vanilla essence
4 egg whites

Filling and icing:
¼ cup (2 oz) castor sugar
1 tbsp cornflour
¼ tsp salt
1 cup (½ pt) milk
1 egg yolk beaten

1 tbsp margarine
1 tsp vanilla essence
2 cups (6 oz) finely
   grated coconut

This is a very exotic looking gâteau with a delicious creamy coconut flavour. Cream the margarine, shortening and sugar until light and fluffy. Fold in the sifted flour, baking powder and salt alternately with the milk and vanilla and beat well. Beat the egg whites until stiff, stir half into the mixture and then fold the second half in gently. Pour into two lightly greased and floured 8" or 9" tins. Bake at 350°F, 180°C, GM 4 for 30-35 minutes until the top of the cake rises up again when lightly pressed.

Filling and icing: To make the cream, mix the sugar, cornflour and salt in a pan and gradually stir in the milk. Bring to the boil stirring constantly and boil for 1 minute over a medium heat. Stir in the beaten egg yolk and cook for 1 more minute. Stir in the margarine and vanilla and allow to cool. When both the cake and the cream are cool, stir ½ cup (1½ oz) of coconut into ⅓ of the cream and use this as the filling to sandwich the two halves together. Spread the rest of the cream over the top and sides of the cake and gently pat the remaining grated coconut evenly all over it.

The gâteau will keep for up to two days if kept chilled.

Pumpkin Tea Bread

½ cup (4 oz) margarine
¾ cup (6 oz) castor sugar
1 egg beaten
1 tsp Angostura Bitters
2 cups (8 oz) plain flour

1 tbsp baking powder
½ tsp salt
1 cup (½ lb) mashed pumpkin
½ cup (3 oz) raisins

Cream the margarine and sugar until light and fluffy. Add the egg and the Angostura Bitters and mix well. Sift the flour, baking powder and salt and then beat it in alternately with the pumpkin until the mixture is smooth. Ensure all the raisins are separated by tossing them in a tablespoonful of flour, then stir them into the mixture. Pour into a lightly greased loaf tin and bake at 375°F, 190°C, GM 5 for about 1 hour until a skewer inserted in the centre comes out clean.

The "milk" of a coconut makes a sweet and refreshing drink. As the coconut ripens this solidifies to form first a jelly and finally the white flesh called "copra".

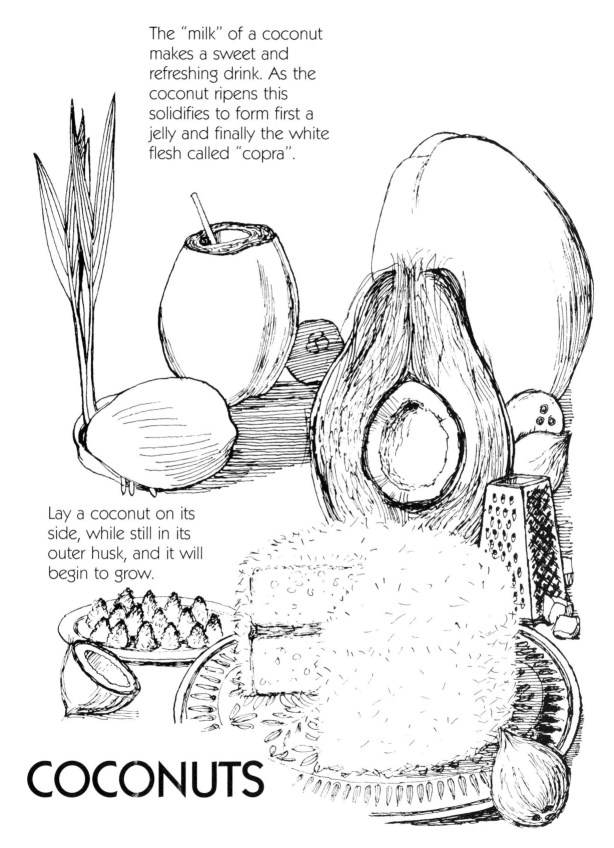

Lay a coconut on its side, while still in its outer husk, and it will begin to grow.

COCONUTS

Caramel Topped Orange Cake

½ cup (4 oz) margarine
1 cup (8 oz) castor sugar
⅔ cup (⅓ pt) orange juice
2 eggs beaten
2 cups (8 oz) plain flour

4 tsp baking powder
¼ tsp salt
Grated rind of 1 orange
3 tbsp (1½ oz) brown sugar

Melt the margarine and pour it over the castor sugar. Beat in the orange juice, eggs, sifted flour, baking powder and salt. Pour into a lightly greased, lined, deep 8″ round tin. Sprinkle with the orange rind and brown sugar and bake at 350°F, 180°C, GM 4 for 1-1¼ hours.

Coconut Bread

½ cup (4 oz) margarine
¼ cup (2 oz) shortening
4 cups (1 lb) self raising flour
½ tsp salt
3 tsp baking powder
¾ cup (6 oz) castor sugar

1 egg
3 tbsp milk
1 tsp vanilla essence
1⅔ cups (5 oz) grated coconut
⅔ cup (4 oz) raisins

Filling:
⅓ cup (1 oz) grated coconut
1 tsp sugar

¼ tsp vanilla essence

This recipe makes two loaves. Melt the margarine and shortening in a small pan. Sift the dry ingredients into a mixing bowl and add the sugar. Lightly whisk the egg and milk together and add to the dry ingredients along with the melted fats, vanilla, coconut and raisins. Knead lightly on a floured surface to mix into a smooth dough, then divide the dough into two equal portions. Roll each half to the length of a loaf tin. Hold half in one hand and make a trough lengthways in the dough with the other hand. Fill the trough with half the filling mixture and then squeeze the edges together to seal. Place in a lightly greased and floured loaf tin, with the sealed edge down. Repeat with the other half of the dough and place it in a second lightly greased and floured loaf tin. Make criss-cross indentations on the top of the loaves with the back of a knife, brush with water and sprinkle with sugar. Bake at 350°F, 180°C, GM 4 for 1¼ hours.

Coconut Pitons

2 egg whites
½ cup (4 oz) brown sugar

2 cups (6 oz) grated coconut
½ tsp almond essence

Whisk the egg whites until stiff, then slowly add the sugar, beating until glossy. Stir in the coconut and almond essence. On a greased baking tray, shape the mixture into 8 peaked shapes, reminiscent of St Lucia's beautiful twin volcanic peaks, Les Pitons. Bake at 325°F, 160°C, GM 3 for 20-25 minutes until light brown all over. Cool on a wire tray.

Fruit Sellers

103

Passion Fruit Swiss Roll

3 eggs
½ cup (4 oz) castor sugar
¾ cup (3 oz) plain flour

½ tsp baking powder
1½ tbsp passion fruit juice

Filling:
¼ cup (2 oz) margarine
1 cup (4 oz) icing sugar

1½ tbsp passion fruit juice

Icing: (optional)
3 tbsp icing sugar

A little passion fruit juice

Beat the eggs and sugar until light and fluffy. Fold in the sifted flour, baking powder and passion fruit juice. Spread the mixture very evenly in a greased and lined 12½″ x 8½″ swiss roll tin. Bake at 400°F, 200°C, GM 6 for about 12 minutes, being careful not to over cook or it will be impossible to roll without cracking it. Turn out onto a well sugared piece of grease proof paper and trim off the crispy edges so the edges are soft sponge. Quickly spread it with the filling and roll it as tightly as possible. Ice when cool, making the icing thin enough to trickle over the swiss roll in a pattern of fine lines.

Coconut Cake

½ cup (4 oz) margarine
½ cup (4 oz) castor sugar
2 eggs beaten
2 cups (8 oz) plain flour

1 tsp baking powder
2 tbsp milk
1⅓ cups (4 oz) grated coconut

Cream the margarine and sugar until light and fluffy then add the eggs and beat well. Fold in the sifted flour, baking powder, milk and most of the coconut. Pour into a lightly greased loaf tin and sprinkle the remaining coconut over the top. Bake for 1¼ hours at 325°F, 160°C, GM 3.

Coconut Meringues

1 cup (3 oz) grated coconut
3 egg whites

¼ tsp cream of tartar
1 cup (8 oz) castor sugar

Grate the coconut finely a few hours ahead of time and spread it thinly to dry out a little. Beat the egg whites and cream of tartar until they are stiff and frothy. Gradually add the sugar a little at a time, beating until soft and glossy. Gently fold in the grated coconut. Shape the mixture into equal portions on a sheet of lightly greased foil on a baking tray. This quantity of mixture makes about 12 large, 18 medium or 24 small meringues. Bake for 1 hour at 275°F, 140°C, GM 1, reducing the time by 10-20 minutes if your meringues are medium or small in size as they will cook faster. When they are cooked turn the oven off and leave the meringues inside until completely cool.

PASSION FRUIT

Sweet Banana Cake

¼ cup (2 oz) margarine
½ cup (4 oz) castor sugar
2 eggs beaten
1 cup (4 oz) plain flour
1 tsp baking powder
½ tsp salt
3 bananas peeled and halved lengthways
Juice of 1 lime or ½ a lemon
⅓ cup (3 oz) brown sugar
⅓ cup (1 oz) grated coconut

Cream the margarine and sugar until light and fluffy, then add the eggs and beat well. Add the sifted flour, baking powder and salt and again beat well. Pour into a lightly greased 8" square tin spreading evenly. Quickly arrange the banana slices on top, sprinkle with the lime or lemon juice, brown sugar and coconut. Bake at 350°F, 180°C, GM 4 for 30-35 minutes. To turn the cake out put a sheet of grease proof paper on a wire tray and turn the cake onto it. Quickly put a second wire tray over the base of the cake and invert again.

Cassava Pone

1 lb cassava
1 cup (3 oz) grated coconut
2 tbsp butter
1 tbsp lard
½ cup (4 oz) brown sugar
1 tsp baking powder
½ tsp mixed essence
½ tsp mixed spice
¼ tsp ground cinnamon
1 tbsp flour

Peel and grate the cassava (sweet potato is an alternative), and mix it with the coconut. Work the butter and lard in with a fork. Add all the remaining ingredients plus 2 table-spoonfuls of water and stir into a stiff mixture. Put into a lightly greased 7" square tin, so that the mixture is 1½-2" deep, and sprinkle with a little brown sugar. Bake at 350°F, 180°C, GM 4 for 1¼ hours until firm and crisp. Cut into 16 squares. Best eaten fresh.

Moist Grapefruit Cake

2 cups (8 oz) plain flour
1 tsp bicarbonate of soda
⅓ cup (3 oz) castor sugar
Grated rind of 1 grapefruit
½ cup (4 oz) margarine
⅓ cup (3 oz) grapefruit marmalade
½ cup (¼ pt) grapefruit juice
1 egg beaten

Topping:
⅓ cup (3 oz) brown sugar
½ cup (¼ pt) grapefruit juice

Sift the dry ingredients into a mixing bowl and add the grapefruit rind. Heat the margarine, marmalade and juice until the margarine has melted. Cool slightly and add to the dry ingredients. Beat well and then beat in the egg. Pour into a greased and lined 7" or 8" square tin. Bake at 325°F, 160°C, GM 3 for 1-1¼ hours. When cooked, cool in the tin for about 10 minutes then turn onto a wire rack with a plate under the rack. To make the topping, heat the sugar and juice until the sugar dissolves, then spoon it over the warm cake. Oranges or lemons can be substituted for the grapefruit ingredients.

CASSAVA

The root of the Cassava plant has been a versatile food since the time of the early inhabitants of the Caribbean, the Arawak and Carib Indians.

The drawing shows how historically the root was grated on a board set with splinters of stone, wood, thorns and coral. It was then squeezed in a basket tube and the juice used to make Tomali sauce, an alcoholic drink called Ouicou, and the food preservative Cassareep. Gratings were also sifted to make a flour for cakes, baked on a clay griddle. (Today about 2,000 Carib descendants live in Dominica).

Jamaican Rum Cake

⅔ cup (4 oz) chocolate chips or dark cooking chocolate
½ cup (4 oz) margarine
1½ cups (12 oz) soft brown sugar
2 eggs separated
⅔ cup (4 oz) raisins chopped

2½ cups (10 oz) self raising flour
Pinch of salt
½ tsp cinnamon
½ cup (¼ pt) sour milk*
3 tbsp rum

Melt the chocolate in a small bowl set in a pan of water over a low heat. Cream the margarine and 1¼ cups (10 oz) of the sugar until light and fluffy. Add the egg yolks, the remaining sugar, raisins and the melted chocolate. Fold in the sifted flour, salt and cinnamon alternately with 3 tablespoonfuls of hot water, the sour milk and the rum. Beat the egg whites until stiff, stir half into the cake mixture and then fold the second half in gently. Pour into a lightly greased 8″ square tin and bake for 50-60 minutes at 350°F, 180°C, GM 4. After taking the cake out of the oven leave it in the tin for 15 minutes before turning it out. This cake can be given a more decorative finish by adding a ring of almond halves and a sprinkling of castor sugar to the top before it is baked.

*To make sour milk add ½ teaspoonful of vinegar or lime juice to ½ cup (¼ pt) of normal room temperature milk. Keep in a warm place for 10 minutes to allow it to curdle.

Coconut Tartlets

¾ cup (3 oz) plain flour
¼ cup (1 oz) cornflour
¼ tsp baking powder
Pinch of salt

¼ cup (2 oz) margarine
¼ cup (2 oz) sugar
1 egg yolk beaten

Filling:
Guava jelly
½ cup (2 oz) ground almonds
⅔ cup (2 oz) grated coconut
½ cup (4 oz) castor sugar

1 tbsp milk
Few drops almond essence
1 egg white

Sift the dry ingredients together then rub in the margarine until the mixture becomes rough and crumbly. Stir in the sugar then add the beaten egg yolk and just enough water to make a dryish dough. Chill the dough for 1 hour then roll out the pastry until it is just under ¼″ thick. Line 8-9 small bun tins using a fluted pastry cutter.

Filling: Put ½ teaspoonful of guava jelly into each pastry case. Mix the other ingredients, folding in the stiffly beaten egg white last. Spoon the mixture on top of the guava jelly and bake at 350°F, 180°C, GM 4 for 15-20 minutes. Makes about 8-9.

Did you know that .....
Increasingly, sugar cane is cut by mechanical harvester rather than by hand.

Cutting Sugar Cane

109

Coconut Squares

1 cup (8 oz) margarine melted
4 eggs beaten
1½ cups (12 oz) light brown sugar
1 tsp vanilla essence
½ tsp salt

2 cups (8 oz) plain flour
1 tsp baking powder
1 cup (3 oz) grated coconut
About 1 cup (4 oz) chopped nuts,
    chocolate chips or chopped dates

Combine the ingredients and beat well before folding in the coconut and the nuts, chocolate chips or dates. Bake in two lightly greased 12½″ x 8½″ swiss roll tins at 325°F, 160°C, GM 3 for about 40 minutes. Cut into squares as it cools and remove from the tins when cold. Makes about 24.

Chocolate Spice Cake

¾ cup (6 oz) margarine
¾ cup (6 oz) castor sugar
1 cup (6 oz) chocolate chips or
    dark cooking chocolate

3 eggs separated
1½ cups (6 oz) self raising flour
2 tsp mixed spice

Icing:
1½ cups (6 oz) icing sugar

Fresh orange juice

Cream the margarine and sugar until light and fluffy. Melt ⅔ cup (4 oz) of the chocolate chips or cooking chocolate, and stir it into the creamed mixture. Stir in the beaten egg yolks, sifted flour, spice and remaining chocolate chips. (If using a bar of cooking chocolate chop it to resemble chocolate chips). Fold in the stiffly beaten egg whites and pour into a lightly greased 8″ square tin. Bake at 350°F, 180°C, GM 4 for about 50 minutes until firm when touched. When cool, ice with an icing made from the combined sifted icing sugar and the orange juice.

Banana Oaties

¾ cup (6 oz) margarine
¾ cup (6 oz) castor sugar
1 egg beaten
2-3 bananas mashed
3½ cups (10 oz) rolled oats
½ cup (2 oz) chopped nuts

1½ cups (6 oz) plain flour
½ tsp bicarbonate of soda
1 tsp salt
¼ tsp ground nutmeg
¾ tsp ground cinnamon

Cream the margarine and sugar until light and fluffy. Beat in the egg, followed by the bananas, rolled oats and nuts. Sift in the flour, bicarbonate of soda, salt and spices and beat well. Place teaspoonfuls of the mixture onto 2 ungreased baking trays, flattening the Oaties slightly and spacing them 1¼″ apart. Bake at 400°F, 200°C, GM 6 for about 15 minutes until lightly browned. Cool for 2-3 minutes then put them on a wire rack to cool.

Coconut Seller

Coconut Cookies

½ cup (4 oz) margarine
½ cup (4 oz) castor sugar
2 eggs beaten
½ tsp vanilla essence

1½ cups (6 oz) plain flour
Pinch of salt
1⅓ cups (4 oz) grated coconut

Cream the margarine and sugar until light and fluffy. Add the beaten eggs and the vanilla and beat well. Fold in the sifted flour and salt and then the coconut. Drop teaspoonfuls of the mixture onto a lightly greased baking tray, spacing them well and flattening them slightly. Bake at 350°F, 180°C, GM 4 for about 10-12 minutes. Makes about 24.

Banana Bread

3 medium bananas
⅓ cup (3 oz) margarine
⅔ cup (6 oz) castor sugar
1 egg beaten

2 cups (8 oz) plain flour
4 tsp baking powder
1 tsp salt

This is a good recipe for using up over-ripe bananas. Liquidise or mash the bananas (liquidising is preferable as it will make the mixture lighter). Cream the margarine and sugar until light and fluffy and then beat in the egg. Beat in the sifted flour, baking powder and salt alternately with the liquidised banana. Bake in a lightly greased loaf tin at 350°F, 180°C, GM 4 for about 1 hour. Banana bread is delicious eaten warm with butter.

Frosted Banana Cup Cakes

4 medium bananas
2 tbsp (1 oz) margarine
1 cup (8 oz) castor sugar

1 egg beaten
1¼ cups (5 oz) plain flour
1½ tsp baking powder

Frosting:
½ medium banana mashed

1½ cups (6 oz) icing sugar

These cup cakes are moist and full of flavour. Liquidise or mash the bananas (liquidising is preferable as it will make the mixture lighter). Cream the margarine and sugar until light and fluffy. Add the egg and liquidised bananas (over-ripe ones are fine). Beat well, then beat in the sifted flour and baking powder. Spoon the mixture into lightly greased and floured bun tins. Bake at 375°F, 190°C, GM 5 for about 20 minutes until risen and browned. Ice with the banana frosting when cool. When making the frosting reserve a little of the banana to add only if the frosting is too stiff to spread smoothly. Makes about 18.

Did you know that .....
Banana trees blow over easily in hurricanes but new suckers will fruit again in a year.

Sauces,
Candies
and Preserves

Tamarind Sauce

3 cups (1½ pts) water
6 large tamarind pods
2 tbsp brown sugar
Cornflour

Tamarinds are a main ingredient in Worcestershire sauce so this has a similar sharp flavour and is good served with all meats. Bring the water to the boil. Shell the tamarinds and add the flesh and seeds to the water. Simmer until reduced by half and the flesh comes off the seeds. Strain to remove the seeds and then return it to the heat. Add the sugar and a little cornflour to thicken the sauce as required. Serves 6.

Paw-Paw Sauce

1 small unripe paw-paw
              (papaya)
1½ cups (¾ pt) water
4 cloves
2 tbsp sugar
Juice of 1 lime or half
              a lemon

This makes a very nice alternative to apple sauce, served with all meats and poultry. Peel and chop the paw-paw and simmer it in the water with all the other ingredients for about an hour. When the paw-paw is soft and most of the water absorbed discard the cloves, sieve the sauce and serve it hot or cold. Serves 6.

Barbados Cherry Sauce

1 cup (½ pt) cherry skins,
       juice and pulp
1 cup (½ pt) water
3 tbsp honey
2 tsp cherry liqueur
       (optional)

Cherry Sauce is a fruity orange colour, delicious served with pork or chicken in the manner of cranberry sauce. To prepare the cherries cut away the fruit and skins, and squeeze the seeds to collect the juice. Cook this with the water for 10 minutes, until the cherry skins are soft. Cool and then liquidise. Stir in the honey, and the cherry liqueur if chosen. Serve hot or cold. Serves 4.

Crystallised Shaddock Rind

Rind of one or more
              shaddocks
½-1 tsp salt
Granulated sugar

Lightly grate off part of the colourful outer rind. Cut off the white pith in large pieces. Weigh the pith (and note the weight for future reference), then soak it in water with the salt, overnight. Next day, rinse it and again top with fresh water and cook until tender. If the dry rind weighed 1 lb, then add 4 cups (2 lb) of sugar and 2 cups (1 pt) of the water in which the skins have been cooked, plus 2 cups (1 pt) of fresh water. Now cook until the water boils away. Squeeze the skins to remove excess water, then cut into bite-sized pieces, shake in granulated sugar and dry on a wire rack.

Carambola, also known as Star fruit, is another fruit to crystallise. Cut it into slices (which will be star shaped), and miss out the stage of soaking it overnight.

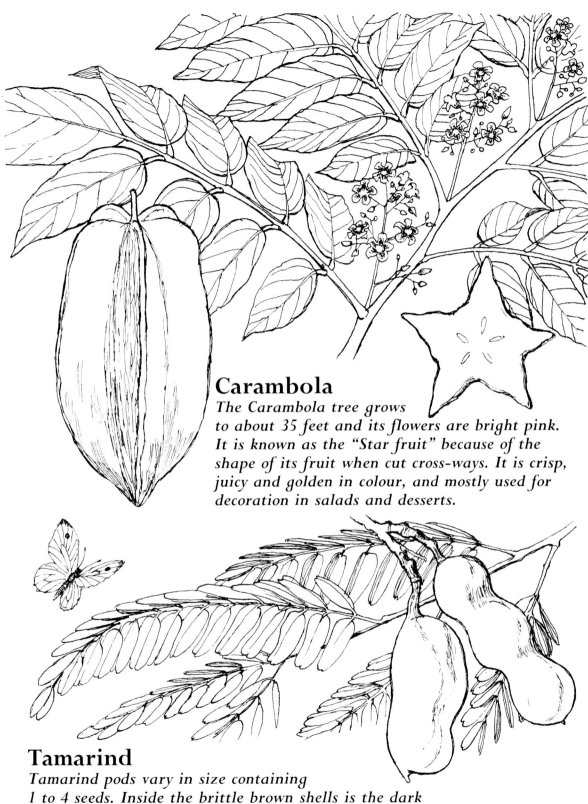

Carambola

*The Carambola tree grows
to about 35 feet and its flowers are bright pink.
It is known as the "Star fruit" because of the
shape of its fruit when cut cross-ways. It is crisp,
juicy and golden in colour, and mostly used for
decoration in salads and desserts.*

Tamarind

*Tamarind pods vary in size containing
1 to 4 seeds. Inside the brittle brown shells is the dark
brown pulp. It is very acid and is not usually eaten raw.
It is a valuable ingredient in chutneys, curries and Worcestershire sauce.*

115

Coconut Sugar Cakes

2½ cups (7½ oz) grated coconut
1½ cups (12 oz) castor sugar

Heat the sugar in ½ cup (¼ pt) of water and when the sugar is dissolved add the coconut. Boil gently, stirring to avoid it burning. Cook until the mixture becomes stiff, then drop spoonfuls onto a moistened baking tray and leave to set. Traditionally half the mixture is made pink by adding a few drops of cochineal. Makes about 12.

Rum Fudge

2 cups (1 lb) white sugar
½ cup (¼ pt) milk
¼ cup (2 oz) margarine
⅔ cup (⅓ pt) condensed milk
½ tsp vanilla essence
1 tbsp rum

Bring the sugar, milk and margarine to the boil in a large pan, stirring frequently. Add the condensed milk and return to the boil. Keep stirring and in about 20 minutes the mixture will form solid droplets when dropped into cold water. Add the vanilla and rum, remove from the heat and stir for 2-3 minutes. Pour into a lightly greased 11" x 7" baking tray to cool. Cut into squares before it is completely set.

Guava Cheese

Guavas
Granulated sugar

Top and tail the guavas and rub both the skin and the flesh through a sieve, discarding the seeds. Weigh the pulp and put it in a pan with the same weight of sugar. Boil until stiff and then turn it into a greased and sugared baking tray to set. When it is cool cut into squares and dust with sugar.

Coconut Truffles

¼ cup (2 oz) margarine
1 cup (4 oz) icing sugar
1 cup (3 oz) grated coconut
⅔ cup (4 oz) chocolate chips

Cream the margarine and icing sugar and then stir in the coconut. Melt the chocolate over hot water. Roll the coconut mixture into marble sized balls and dip into the melted chocolate. Place on a baking tray and chill until hard. Store in the fridge. Delicious with after-dinner coffee!

Rum Truffles

1 cup (6 oz) chocolate chips
¼ cup (2 oz) margarine
2 egg yolks beaten
2 tbsp rum
Ground almonds

Melt the chocolate chips over hot water and allow to cool a little. Stir in the margarine, egg yolks and rum and chill until the mixture is firm enough to shape. Roll into marble sized balls and then roll in the ground almonds. Alternative coatings are chocolate sugar strands or sieved icing sugar. Store in the fridge.

Caribbean
Coconut Palms

Guava Jelly

Guavas
Granulated sugar
Lime or lemon juice

Guava jelly is an attractive deep amber shade. Wash and chop the guavas, put in a large pan and cover with water. Boil uncovered until the guavas are soft and the water a little reduced, about 15-20 minutes. Strain off the juice, measure and return it to the pan with the same volume of sugar. Stir and bring to the boil, skimming it occasionally. Add 1 teaspoonful of lime or lemon juice to every 25 guavas. The jelly is ready after about 5 minutes of fast boiling or when a teaspoonful dropped onto a cool plate forms a jelly.

Cherry Jam

Barbados cherries
Granulated sugar

Prepare the cherries as in Barbados Cherry Jelly (see page 94). Weigh the fruit and simmer for about 20 minutes, until soft. Add the same weight of sugar and cook for about 20 minutes until a teaspoonful dropped on a plate cools to the right consistency. Mango jam can be made in the same way.

Mammey Apple Jam

1 medium mammey apple
1 cinnamon stick
Granulated sugar

Cut off the outer skin and pith to reveal the mammey apple's orange flesh. Cut the flesh into pieces, put in a pan with the cinnamon stick and just cover with water. Cook for 5 minutes until partly tender, then measure the quantity and add half its volume in sugar. Put the fruit and sugar back in the pan and cook for a further 20 minutes until the fruit is soft and a light syrup forms. Makes about one jar of jam.

Spicy Mango Chutney

8 cups (2 lbs) peeled and
  chopped green mango
4 cups (2 lbs) sugar
1½ cups (¾ pt) white
  vinegar
1 tsp salt
⅓ cup (2 oz) prunes
⅓ cup (2 oz) raisins
⅓ cup (2 oz) currants
3" fresh ginger
2 cloves garlic
1 bonnie pepper

This is a very handy recipe for making good use of the unripe mangoes which fall at the beginning of the mango season. Put the mango, sugar, vinegar and salt in a large pan. Chop the prunes, raisins and currants and add them. Peel and grate the ginger and add it, along with the crushed garlic. Seed and chop the bonnie pepper before adding it. (When chopping bonnie peppers hold them with a knife and fork as they make the skin burn). Bring to the boil and cook for 30 minutes, stirring occasionally, until the chutney is thick. Cool and pour into sterilised jars.

Drinks

Jimmy's Rum Punch

¼ cup (2 oz) brown sugar
4   8 fl oz bottles tonic
        or bitter lemon
Juice of 3 limes or
            2 lemons
1 cup (½ pt) rum
Ground nutmeg
Cucumber sliced

Combine the sugar, 3 bottles of tonic or bitter lemon, the lime or lemon juice and rum. Stir to dissolve the sugar then chill. Later add ice and the last tonic or bitter lemon, sprinkle with ground nutmeg and add the slices of cucumber to remove the sweetness. Serves 6.
A delicious drink which is stronger than one anticipates!

Rum Cocktail

4 fl oz rum
½ cup (¼ pt) crushed ice
3 dashes Angostura
            Bitters
2 tsp sugar syrup or
    Falernum (optional)

This was the sugar planter's traditional drink. Put all the ingredients into a cocktail shaker and shake well. Pour into cocktail glasses. Serves 4.

Daiquiri

6-8 fl oz rum
¼ cup (2 oz) sugar
Juice of 2 limes or
            1 lemon
1 tsp egg white (optional)

This recipe uses a 3 cup (1½ pt) cocktail shaker. Fill the shaker to just below the top with crushed ice. Pour in enough rum to come near the top of the ice. Add the sugar, lime or lemon juice and egg white, shake well and serve quickly while still frothy. Serves 4.

Fruit Daiquiris

1½ fl oz rum
1 tsp lime or lemon juice
3 tsp sugar
Small quantity of fruit
Flowers to garnish

The choice of fruit is unlimited but suggestions include one of the following: half a banana, two tablespoonfuls of passion fruit or cherry juice, or three tablespoonfuls of guava purée. Put all the ingredients into a liquidiser and blend until frothy. Pour into cocktail glasses over crushed ice and garnish with the flowers. Serves 2.

Diamond Rock Coffee

8 tsp instant coffee
½ cup (¼ pt) condensed
            milk
6 tbsp rum
Sugar (optional)

Diamond Rock is a 575ft outcrop off Martinique. During the Napoleonic Wars British sailors fought from it for 17 months. Dissolve the coffee in a little boiling water and fill up to 2 cups (1 pt) with cold water. Stir in the remaining ingredients and pour over large ice cubes to chill. Serves 4-6.

Thirstquenchers for all !

Passion Fruit Sunset

3 tbsp passion fruit juice
   or granadilla juice
4 tbsp white rum
1 tbsp evaporated milk
Ground nutmeg

Blend the juice, rum and evaporated milk in a liquidiser for 30 seconds. Pour into a large glass filled with crushed ice and sprinkle with nutmeg. Serves 1.

Pina Colada

1 cup (½ pt) crushed ice
4 tbsp pineapple juice
2 tbsp cream of coconut
2 tbsp rum
Pineapple & Maraschino
   cherry to garnish

Put the ice into a cocktail shaker or blender and add all the other ingredients. Blend for 30 seconds, pour into a tall glass and garnish with the pineapple and cherry. Then sit back, sip it and relax! Serves 1.

Sorrel Drink

Sorrel
Orange peel, cloves
     or cinnamon
Granulated sugar

This recipe is for red sorrel, but there is also a white sorrel which is more acid, so for that allow more water. Cut the red sepals from the sorrel and discard the outside frill and seed. Dry for 1 day. Put the sepals into a bowl and cover with hot water and add a choice of the spices. Cover and leave for another day. Strain off the liquid and measure it, adding ½ cup (4 oz) of sugar to every 2 cups (1 pt) of liquid. Serve chilled with ice. This is a clear red drink, traditionally served at Christmas time.

Mauby

4 pieces mauby bark
     – 3" long
Small piece dried
     orange peel
1" piece cinnamon stick
3-4 cloves
1 blade mace
2 cups (1 lb) brown sugar
9 cups (4½ pts) water
½ tsp mixed essence

In days gone by a "Mauby Lady" sold cups of mauby from a tall can with a tap which she carried on her head. The bark used in the drink comes from a small shrubby tree, mainly found in Haiti and the Dominican Republic. Boil the mauby bark in 1 cup (½ pt) of water for about 5 minutes, along with the dried orange peel, cinnamon, cloves and mace, then cool. Dissolve the sugar in 2 cups (1 pint) of hot water, then add it and the remaining 6 cups (3 pints) of cold water to the mauby, along with the mixed essence. Strain the mauby into bottles, filling only to the shoulder of each bottle, so that the entire neck of the bottle is left for froth. Put tops on the bottles and leave for 3 days. Serve chilled with ice. Mauby keeps best if the sugar is added just prior to drinking.

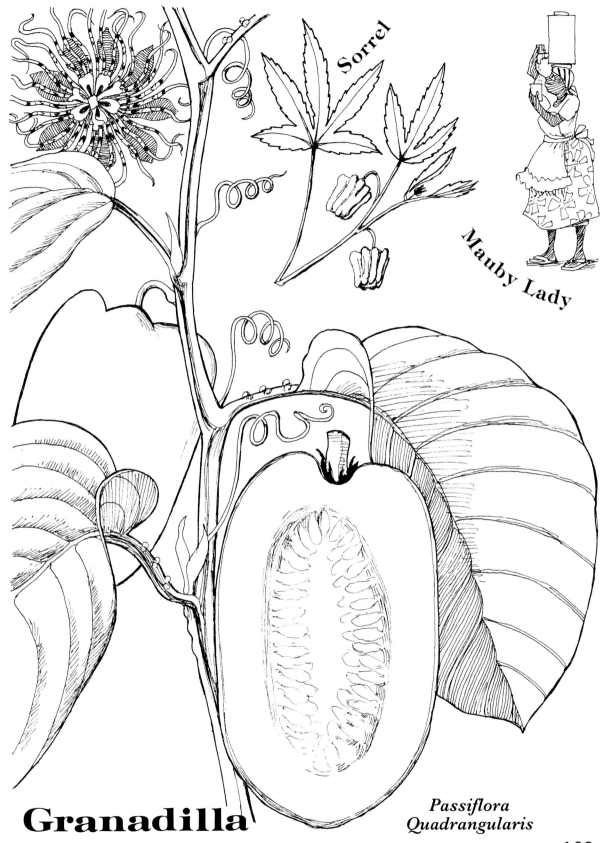

Sorrel

Mauby Lady

Granadilla

Passiflora Quadrangularis

Soursop Cooler

1 medium soursop
1½ cups (¾ pt) water
½ cup (¼ pt) condensed milk
3 tbsp castor sugar
Some colourful flowers

Despite its name, soursop is not at all sour. It look like a huge dark green strawberry and its flesh is pure white. Peel the soursop and crush the flesh with a potato masher. Boil the water and add half to the soursop. Sieve to remove the soursop seeds and then stir in the remaining water, condensed milk and sugar. Chill and serve with ice, decorated with a colourful long stemmed flower. Serves 6-8. Relax when drinking soursop as it has a soporific effect!

Guava Ice-Cap

1 cup (8 oz) guava shells (peeled and de-seeded)
3 tbsp honey
2 cups (1 pt) milk

Simmer the guava shells with the honey and a few tablespoonfuls of water for about 10 minutes to soften the guavas. Liquidise, and then add the milk. Blend in the liquidiser until frothy. Quickly pour it over lots of crushed ice and serve. Serves 6.

Tropical Milk Shake

½ small paw-paw (papaya), peeled and de-seeded
1 banana
1 cup (½ pt) milk
1 tbsp honey

Liquidise the paw-paw and banana and then add the milk and the honey. Blend again and quickly pour this creamy refresher over lots of crushed ice and serve. Serves 1 large glass or 2 small glasses.

Paradise Cooler

1 medium mango
1 tbsp lime or lemon juice
½ cup (¼ pt) soda water
A little honey or sugar
Lime or lemon slices

Chop the mango flesh roughly and then liquidise it along with the lime or lemon juice. Pour into one large or two small glasses and top up with soda and ice and stir well. Sweeten to taste and stir again. Garnish the glasses with slices of lime or lemon. Serves 1 large glass or 2 small glasses.

Pirate Liqueur

1 tbsp instant coffee
1 cup (8 oz) sugar
1 cup (½ pt) water
2 tsp vanilla essence
1 cup (½ pt) rum
1½ tbsp brandy

This is a strong, dark coffee liqueur. Bring the coffee, sugar and water to the boil, stirring to dissolve the sugar. Reduce the heat and simmer uncovered for 3 minutes. Remove from the heat and when it is luke-warm add the vanilla, rum and brandy. Pour into a sterilised bottle, seal and keep in a cool, dark cupboard for 2 weeks · a long wait!

aah. . . . . .that *dream* drink !

Index

Index

Jill Walker's

CARIBBEAN COOKBOOK

Featuring 52 Jill Walker Drawings

Written by Charlotte Hingston with illustrations by Jill Walker

Acknowledgements

Susan Trew   First, we would like to give a special thanks to Jill Walker's youngest daughter, Susan Trew, who helped greatly with gathering and selecting the recipes. This was no small task!

We would also like to thank the following people for their kind assistance with the recipes: Edla Adams, Cynthia Bradshaw, Sarah & Darryl Cobb, Brigitte Lafosse-Marin, Carmeta Fraser, Shirley Hooper, Marjorie Lander, Jenny Lopez, Andrea MacKenzie, Didi Mudd, Jimmy & Claudina Pastoriza, Chris Trew, Maurice & Vivien Trew, Carolyn Woodroffe.

Rear Cover Photo   The photograph of Jill Walker in her studio in Barbados was taken by Ronnie Carrington for an article on Best of Barbados Limited in "Options" Magazine. The photo is reproduced with their kind permissions.

Published by Best of Barbados Limited, Welches, St. Thomas, Barbados.
        Tel: (246) 421 6900 Fax: (246) 421 6393
        e-mail: sales@best-of-barbados.com

Typeset in News Gothic with headings in Benguiat.
Printed in Singapore.
ISBN 0 906555 07 8